Come Sunday

Front Cover Top:

- The ancestor tree is one of several names in oral history for the largest, and perhaps oldest, tree in the square. It is often the center of prayers as well as spiritual altars and offerings.
- The circular-patterned paving stones that cover the ground of Congo Square and other renovations of the location were completed in 1980 in time for the opening of Louis Armstrong Park.
- The dancing feet that appear on the cover and at the beginning of each chapter represent the people of African heritage who gathered in Congo Square on Sunday afternoons to celebrate their cultural heritage.

Front Cover Bottom:

Left: An elderly woman wearing a tignon head wrap walking in Congo Square, February 1891. This is one of the oldest known photos of the historical landmark.

Center: FiYiYi Mandingo Warrior Big Chief Victor Harris teaching boys at a Sunday gathering in Congo Square, March 10, 2013. This is an example of passing on culture.

Right: A painting of a Calinda dance in the Caribbean by François Aimé Louis Dumoulin. This dance and the drumming style, where the drummer straddles the drum, were prevalent in Congo Square and other locations in New Orleans. This is an example of the parallel cultural practices that existed in parts of Africa, the Caribbean, and New Orleans.

Printed on acid-free paper in the United States

Library of Congress Cataloging-in-Publication Data

Names: Evans, Freddi Williams, author. | Adaptation of (work): Evans, Freddi Williams. Congo square.
Title: Come Sunday : a young reader's history of Congo Square / by Freddi Williams Evans.
Description: Lafayette, LA : University of Louisiana at Lafayette Press, 2017. | Originally published as: Congo Square : African roots in New Orleans. Lafayette, LA : University of Louisiana at Lafayette Press, 2011. | Audience: Grades 4 to 6. | Includes bibliographical references and index.
Identifiers: LCCN 2017030672 | ISBN 9781946160102
Subjects: LCSH: Congo Square (New Orleans, La.)--History--Juvenile literature. | African Americans--Louisiana--New Orleans--Social life and customs--Juvenile literature. | African Americans--Louisiana--New Orleans--Music--History and criticism--Juvenile literature. | African American dance--Louisiana--New Orleans--History--Juvenile literature. | Community life--Louisiana--New Orleans--History--Juvenile literature. | New Orleans (La.)--History--Juvenile literature. | New Orleans (La.)--Social life and customs--Juvenile literature.
Classification: LCC F379.N57 C662 2017 | DDC 976.3/35--dc23
LC record available at https://lccn.loc.gov/2017030672

Come Sunday

A Young Reader's History of Congo Square

Freddi Williams Evans

2017
University of Louisiana at Lafayette Press

Table of Contents

Introduction

Ba-doom! Ba-doom! Ba-doom, doom, doom.
Ba-doom! Ba-doom! Ba-doom, doom, doom.

On Sunday afternoons in Congo Square, drumbeats echoed like dancing thunder, calling people to gather. Enslaved men, women, boys, and girls responded by the hundreds, sometimes thousands. With quick steps and wide strides, they cut across empty lots and hurried along narrow paths to the open space back-of-town. They came from "uptown," "front-of-town," and "out-of-town" to a place where they could lay slavery down. They came to play music, sing, dance, buy and sell, practice religions, and speak the languages that they learned in their homelands.

Hundreds of people came to watch. For them, the gatherings were entertainment; but, for those who were enslaved, they were a few hours of partial freedom. The enslaved were free to come together and free to keep their culture alive. They were free to be themselves.

Sainville, an enslaved boy who lived and worked near Congo Square, no doubt attended some of those gatherings. When he ran away from his owner on February 12, 1856, the owner placed the announcement or runaway ad, at right, in the newspaper offering a reward to anyone who would return Sainville.

Through the years, writers used a variety of terms to refer to black people who were held in bondage, and the documents in this book contain some of them, including slave, colored, griff (griffe), mulatto, mulatress, Negro, negro, and negress. The author of this book uses the term "enslaved." It infers that people in powerful positions placed other people in bondage and called them slaves.

Front–of-town: Vieux Carré means old square and refers to the area within the bordering streets of Canal, Rampart, Esplanade, and Old Levee (now Decatur)

Up-town: The area up-river of Canal Street

Back-of-town: The area behind Rampart Street

Out-of-town: Outside of the city limits

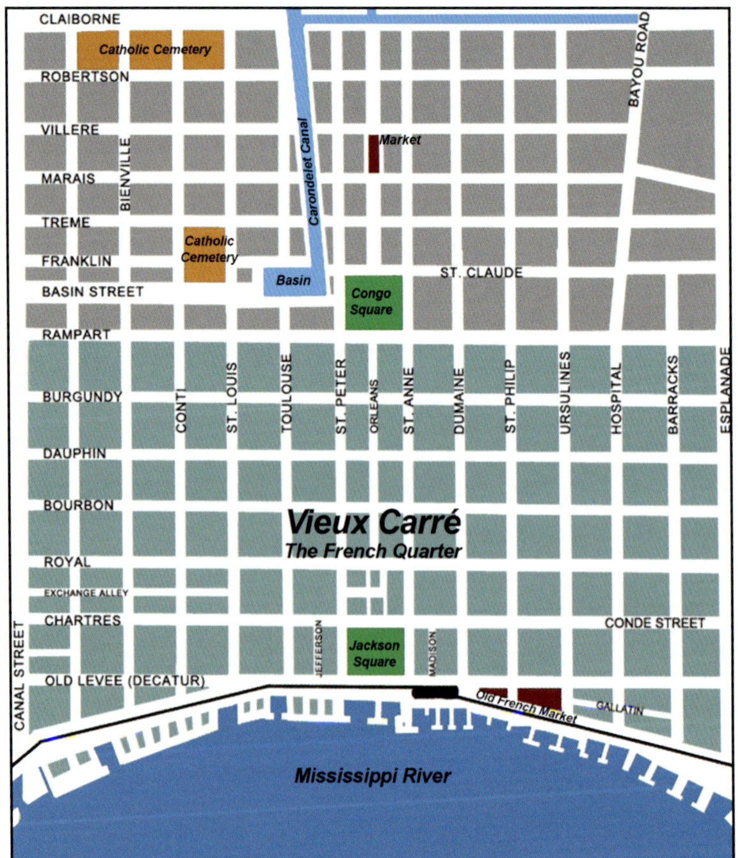

Reproduction of an 1845 map of New Orleans

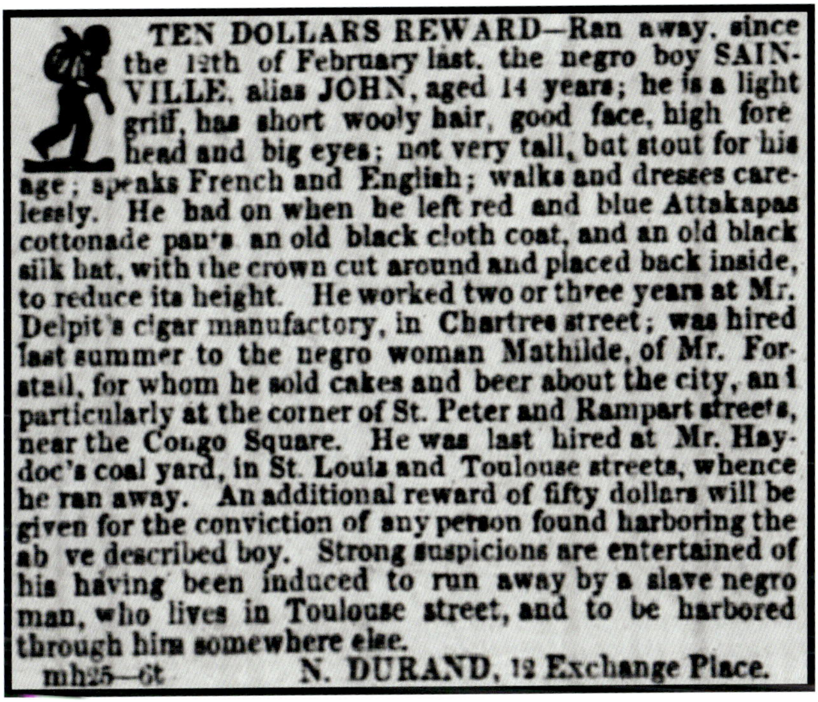

TEN DOLLARS REWARD—Ran away, since the 12th of February last, the negro boy SAINVILLE, alias JOHN, aged 14 years; he is a light griff, has short wooly hair, good face, high fore head and big eyes; not very tall, but stout for his age; speaks French and English; walks and dresses carelessly. He had on when he left red and blue Attakapas cottonade pants, an old black cloth coat, and an old black silk hat, with the crown cut around and placed back inside, to reduce its height. He worked two or three years at Mr. Delpit's cigar manufactory, in Chartres street; was hired last summer to the negro woman Mathilde, of Mr. Forstall, for whom he sold cakes and beer about the city, and particularly at the corner of St. Peter and Rampart streets, near the Congo Square. He was last hired at Mr. Haydoc's coal yard, in St. Louis and Toulouse streets, whence he ran away. An additional reward of fifty dollars will be given for the conviction of any person found harboring the above described boy. Strong suspicions are entertained of his having been induced to run away by a slave negro man, who lives in Toulouse street, and to be harbored through him somewhere else.

mh25—6t N. DURAND, 12 Exchange Place.

Runaway ad for Sainville from the *Daily Picayune*, March 27, 1856

The sankofa symbol, seen above and at the beginning of each chapter, has origins in Africa. It means to "go back and get it" and to "learn from the past." This Adinkra symbol from Ghana, West Africa, appears in ironwork across New Orleans. It even appears in work at the top of the St. Louis Cathedral. Another symbol for sankofa is a bird with its head turned backwards, often taking an egg off its back.

Today, this announcement provides pieces of information about what life was like for some enslaved boys and girls in New Orleans. It gives Sainville's age, what he looked like, and what he was wearing when he left. Sainville was described as a *griff* (also *griffe*), a term that referred to mixed racial parentage and skin color. He was fourteen years old and spoke French and English. His ability to speak French suggests that he probably grew up and was likely born in New Orleans. Sainville had been hired-out, meaning that his owner received money when Sainville worked different jobs around the city. Sainville's owner no doubt gave him a pass, a written document that permitted him to move around the city without landing in jail. His owner once hired him out to work for a woman who was also enslaved but who ran a business and hired others to work for her. The announcement shows some of the jobs that enslaved people worked, how people lived and worked with each oth-

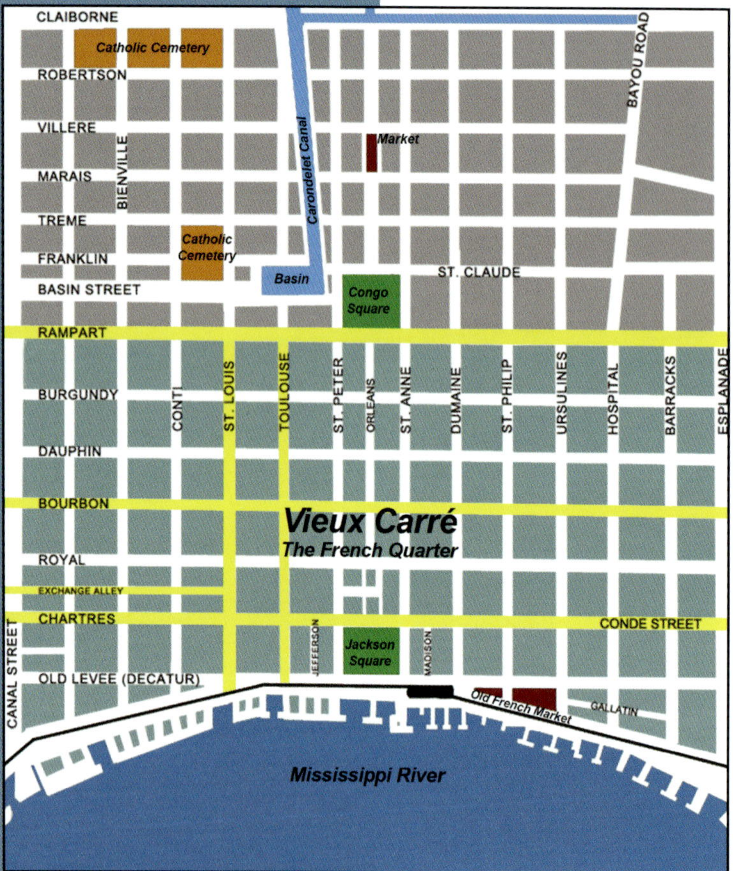

Reproduction of an 1845 map of New Orleans with streets highlighted to show Sainville's footprints in the city

er, and how those who ran away may have received help.

The map at left shows the part of the city where Sainville lived and worked. It identifies the streets mentioned in the runaway ad (i.e. Chartres, St. Peter, Rampart, St. Louis, Toulouse, and Exchange Place). Sainville probably lived with his owner on Exchange Place (also called Exchange Alley), which, at that time, was a narrow path that led from Canal Street to the St. Louis Hotel, one of the prominent locations in the city for slave auctions. Slave traders marched tens of thousands of enslaved people in chains through the alley to and from the auction block. Today, the Louisiana Supreme Court Building, completed in 1910, sits on the block of Exchange Alley that connected it to the hotel. An outline of streets named in the runaway ad for Sainville, including Exchange Alley and the location of Congo Square, provides a view of his footpath in the city.

The runaway ad and the map presented here are among the many primary documents in this book. Enslaved people resisted slavery on an ongoing basis and in different ways, including running away from their slaveholders or owners. Runaway ads, like this one, were the efforts of owners to regain their "property," which they used to make money and build wealth. Today, like windows into the past, these runaway ads and documents allow readers to get as close as possible to what life was like during the time of the gatherings in Congo Square. Photographs, newspaper ads, city laws called ordinances, eyewitness reports, rhythmic patterns, and song lyrics enable readers to analyze, compare, and think critically about the information presented. This process develops a deeper understanding of the people and events that shaped the history of New Orleans's Congo Square.

Right: An elderly woman wearing a tignon head wrap walking in Congo Square, February 1891. This is one of the oldest known photos of the historical landmark.

Left: Old slave block in the St. Louis Hotel, c. 1906

1

History of the Location

The history of the area known as Congo Square includes the Native Americans who inhabited the land and whose ancestors lived in the Mississippi River Valley for more than a thousand years before people from Europe arrived. It also includes the Frenchmen who explored the area in 1699 and those who came to live there after the founding of the city in 1718. The study of Congo Square through the years shows that by the city's one hundredth birthday in 1818, the location had become the only approved Sunday gathering place for enslaved people. Some black people who were free, known as free people of color, gathered with them. A number of additional events made this a popular place for many people in New Orleans.

Before New Orleans

The Mississippi River Valley includes land along the Mississippi River and its tributaries. It stretches over 2,000 miles from northern Minnesota to the mouth of the river below New Orleans at the Gulf of Mexico. The river valley was home to numerous Native American tribes before Europeans arrived. It served as the western boundary of the United States before the Louisiana Purchase of 1803, which added the entire valley to the nation.

Native Americans were the first inhabitants of the land that became New Orleans. Several tribes or nations existed, and some of their members camped on the high and dry ridge along Bayou St. John, which included what is now Congo Square. Some of them reportedly held their corn festivals in the area of Congo Square, which made the location a place of gatherings and celebrations even before the founding of the city. The first play written in Louisiana, in 1809, revealed that those festivals were religious in nature. Today, some Native Americans consider Congo Square to be sacred or holy. Many African Americans also consider it to be sacred because of the historic gatherings of enslaved people that took place there.

The painting, *Dessein de Sauvages de Plusieurs Nations*, or *Drawings of Several Native Americans of Various Nations*, by French artist Alexandre de Batz, is one of the earliest draw-

Map of the United States and Mississippi River Valley territory gained through the Louisiana Purchase

Drawings of Several Native Americans of Various Nations, a painting by Alexandre de Batz, 1735

ings of Native Americans in Louisiana. The title written at the top of the painting specifies New Orleans. Created in 1735, it shows the chief of the Tunica nation, Bride les Bouefs, in war paint holding scalps. Two other subjects are also in war paint, and there is a black child who may or may not have been enslaved. Some black people did live among Native Americans as free people, however, some black people were captured and enslaved by Native Americans. De Batz included members of the Acolapissa, Choctaw, and Natchez nations in his paintings as well. Additional nations that camped in the New Orleans area included the Chapitoulas, Chickasaw, Chitimacha, and Houma.

The historical record of the Tunica tribe, also known as the Tunica-Biloxi tribe, begins with Hernando de Soto's expedition in 1541. It is one of four Native American tribes in Louisiana recognized by the federal government, which makes it eligible to receive services from the United States Bureau of Indian Affairs.

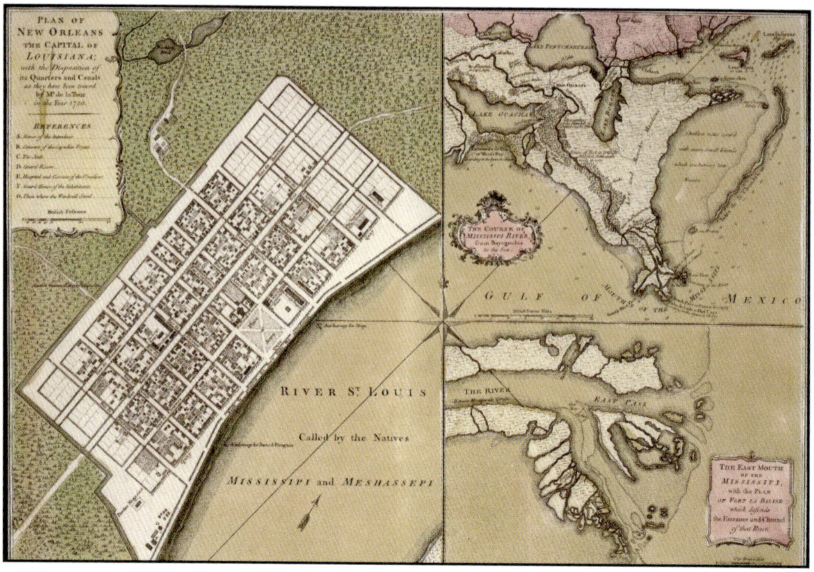

Map showing plan of early New Orleans and Indian portage trail, 1720

Spanish explorer Hernando de Soto arrived in what became Louisiana in 1541. It was French explorer René Robert Cavelier de La Salle, however, who claimed the region and named it Louisiana in 1682 to honor France's King Louis XIV.

A path that members of those nations traveled in and out of the area was called the Indian portage. It connected the Gulf of Mexico and Lake Pontchartrain to Bayou St. John and the Mississippi River. On March 9, 1699, a Native American who had traveled the route many times guided French explorer Jean-Baptiste Le Moyne de Bienville and his crew along the path. Bienville's brother, Pierre Le Moyne, Sieur d'Iberville, was also a crewmember. They traveled from the gulf, to the lake, to the bayou, and then along the Indian portage to the Mississippi River.

The explorers did not remain in the area at that time. Under Iberville's leadership, a settlement for Louisiana was built along the Mississippi Gulf Coast, which was also French territory. In 1718, however, Bienville returned to the place near the crescent-shaped bend in the river where the Indian portage ended. There he founded the city of New Orleans. The marker to the left, located across from Jackson Square near Café Du Monde, pinpoints the place.

Historic marker for the founding of New Orleans

Early Congo Square

During the early years of the city, Bienville and other Frenchmen built homes and businesses along Bayou St. John on the high ground and dry land that had attracted Native Americans. One of those businesses was a brickyard built in 1720 to make bricks to build the city. When Adrian de Pauger made the first plan for New Orleans, he laid out the streets so that the brickyard and area that is Congo Square remained outside the city limits. That area came to be called "back of town." In 1760, city leaders increased the size of New Orleans. They built a fort in the rear of the city, along what is now Rampart Street, to guard the area and brought it inside the city limits. Under Spanish rule the fort at the rear of the city was redesigned and named Fort St. Ferdinand.

The opportunity for enslaved people to assemble on Sundays, which had begun under French rule, continued under the Spanish. Records from the Spanish show that in the 1780s, some enslaved people assembled and danced on the main plaza (now Jackson Square) as well as on the "green expanse," referring to the vicinity of what is now Congo Square. Some visitors to the city who kept journals wrote that they witnessed assembled enslaved people dancing, drumming, and fiddling at other locations as well. In 1797, Francis Baily observed them in the streets and on the green. Two years later, Fortescue Cumming witnessed a gathering on the levee. In 1804, John Watson also observed dancing on the levee.

Spanish officials built Fort Ferdinand in 1792. It was one of five forts surrounding the city of New Orleans. Other forts included Fort St. Jean, Fort Bourgogne, Fort San Luis, and Fort San Carlos. The two largest forts were placed at the edge of the river, and the three others were placed at the back of the city, as seen on the map below.

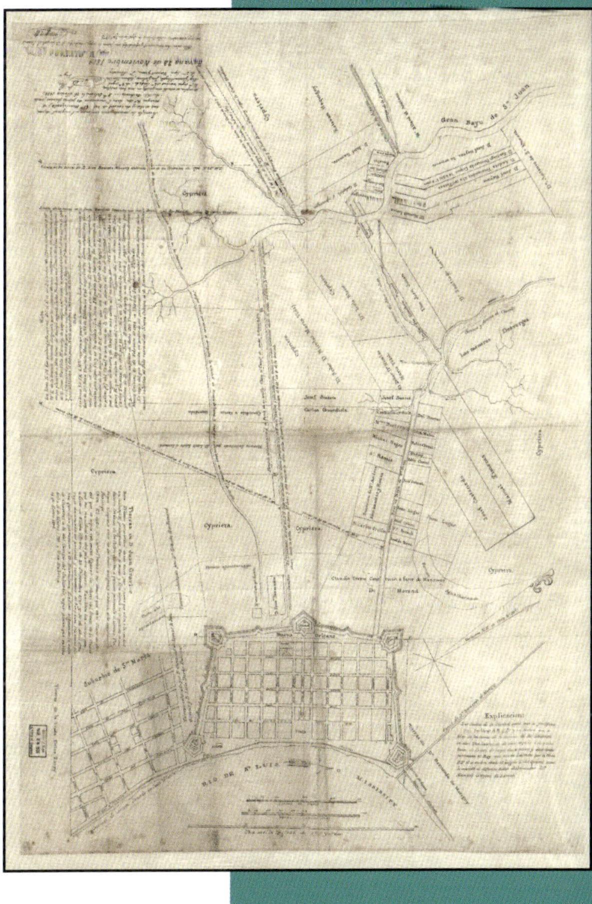

Map of New Orleans under Spanish rule

Flag raising in the Place d'Armes of New Orleans on December 20, 1803; marking the transfer of Louisiana from France to the United States

After the American purchase of Louisiana in 1803, city officials tore down Fort St. Ferdinand, which stimulated the growth and development of the area. Christian Schultz witnessed a gathering at the location in 1803. In 1810, during a city council discussion, Mayor Nicholas Girod mentioned the location near the basin (Carondelet Canal) where enslaved people commonly gathered and danced. The trade of enslaved people within the country and Louisiana's inclusion as the eighteenth state in the American union in 1812 steadily increased the arrival of new residents and visitors. Some of them were so amazed by the Sunday social scene in the city and the gatherings of enslaved black people that they wrote about these events in their journals or travel logs.

The Carondelet Canal, also called the Old Basin Canal, was a 1.6 mile waterway that stretched from Bayou St. John to back-of-town New Orleans—along the edge of Congo Square. It allowed boats to bring products and passengers into the city via Lake Pontchartrain and was navigable from 1794 into the 1920s—nearly 135 years.

A charcoal boat in the Carondelet Canal, c. 1906

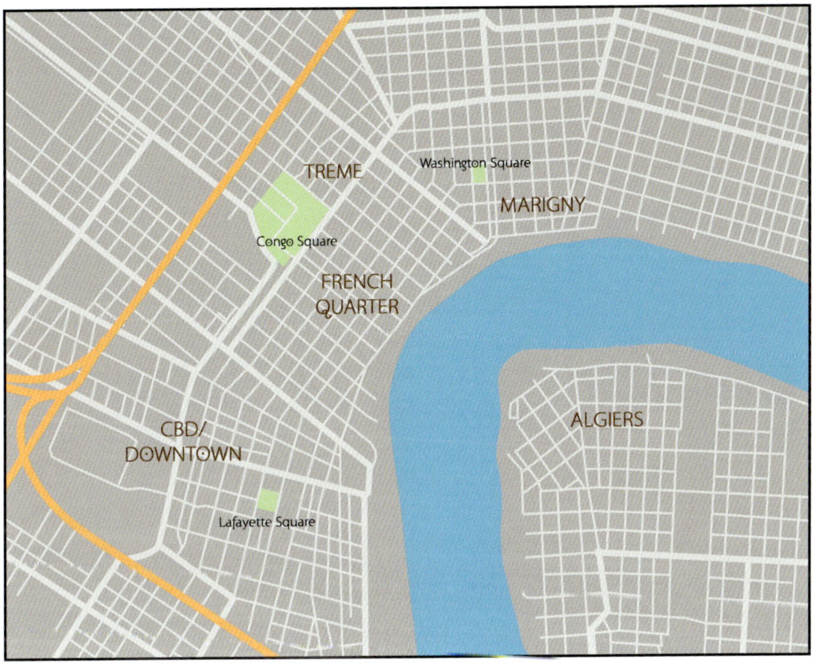

Map of New Orleans locating
Congo Square, Washington Square, and Lafayette Square

With population growth and the city's development came tighter controls on the Sunday gatherings. In 1813, Mayor Girod proposed three locations for enslaved people to gather on Sundays with Congo Square being one of them. The other two were Lafayette Square in the Faubourg Saint Marie neighborhood and Washington Square in Faubourg Marigny. In 1817, the city council again passed an ordinance for the mayor to appoint locations for enslaved people to gather, but those appointments have not been found. However, after that date, Sunday gatherings were only reported from one of those locations—Congo Square.

Other events took place at the location on Sundays as well as through the week. Native Americans held footraces and played a ballgame called racquettes in Congo Square. Black people as well as white people played also.

Residents' and visitors' accounts of Congo Square:

"The Sabbath is devoted to recreation. On this day, the negroes assemble and amuse themselves and spectators by dancing."

–Estwick Evans, June 1818

"On Sabbath evening, the African slaves meet on the green, by the swamp, and rock the city with their Congo dances."

–Henry Cogswell Knight (Arthur Singleton), 1819

"[Congo Square was] very noted on account of its being the place where the Congo and other negroes dance, carouse, and debauch on the Sabbath."

–Norman Paxton's *New Orleans Register & Directory*, 1822 and 1823

"Those who engage in cock fighting were obliged to go to the Congo ground."

–*New Orleans Bee*, September 24, 1831

The Review Yesterday.

The Legion, under Brig. Gen. Palfrey, comprising the Battalion (some five hundred in number) of Artillery; the German Battalion, consisting of five or six companies, with a fine band; the Emmet Guards, Capt. Castell, and the company of Carbineers of 1814–15; and Col. Forno's Battalion, composed of the Washington Artillery, Capt. Soria, the Louisiana Grays, Capt. Cavanagh, and companies A, B, C, D and E of the National Guards, were reviewed yesterday afternoon at the new Place d'Armes, Congo Square, by Major Gen. Lewis, and inspected by Inspector General Forstall, in the presence of a large concourse of spectators. It was apparently completely satisfactory to all who witnessed it.

The Louisiana Grays, with Old Jordan tapping his well worn drum at their head, turned out in good numbers, and made a fine appearance and, in fact, so did all the commands we have above named. The Louisiana Legion met the Guards and the Grays at the entrance of the place of review, and when the whole were assembled, the spectacle was very imposing.

"The Review Yesterday," *Daily Picayune*, August 5, 1854

Animal fights, horse shows, circus shows, firework exhibitions, air balloon shows, and carriage shows all took place there, and Chinese people who lived in the area flew kites there. Some people were punished at the site in a device called a pillory, and some were hanged there. For black people, Congo Square was a place of happiness as well as a place of sorrow and sadness.

In 1850, the location received the official name of Place d'Armes and became the main location for military drills, which previously took place on the main plaza at the front of town (now Jackson Square). An 1854 newspaper article tells about one of those events. There were large military groups like Brig Palfrey's unit of some five hundred men as well as smaller units like the Louisiana Grays, which had "Old Jordan" as its drummer.

Of African descent, Jordan B. Noble, known as "Old Jordan," served as the drummer for Andrew Jackson during the Battle of New Orleans when he was fourteen years old and enslaved. The battle, which took place in 1815, was the last battle in the War of 1812. The American victory over the powerful and well-equipped Royal Navy and Army of Great Britain enabled the United States to expand trade and territory and tremendously boosted confidence and pride among American citizens. While hundreds of other black people, enslaved and free, served during the Battle of New Orleans, Noble was the only black person attached to the 7th regiment, where he

Born in 1800, Jordan Bankston Noble served in three additional wars after the War of 1812, but he did not gain his freedom until his late 30s.

One of the drums that Jordan Noble played in military drills

served directly under General Jackson. Units of free men of color did exist during the battle and at other points in time, and Jordan no doubt drilled with them. Newspaper articles starting in the 1850s tell of his marching in January 8th Day parades with other free men of color who were veterans of the war. At the same time, he continued to serve as the drummer for white military units and some scholars believe that the Louisiana Grays was one of them.

Elderly Jordan Bankston Noble (1800-1890)

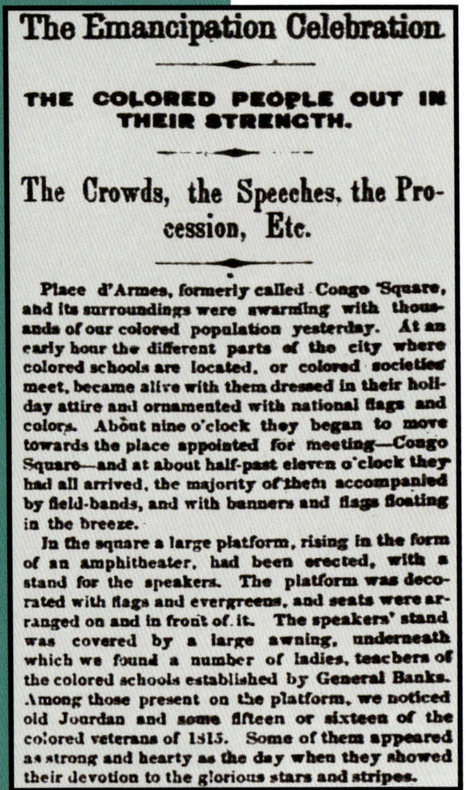

The Emancipation Celebration.

THE COLORED PEOPLE OUT IN THEIR STRENGTH.

The Crowds, the Speeches, the Procession, Etc.

Place d'Armes, formerly called Congo Square, and its surroundings were swarming with thousands of our colored population yesterday. At an early hour the different parts of the city where colored schools are located, or colored societies meet, became alive with them dressed in their holiday attire and ornamented with national flags and colors. About nine o'clock they began to move towards the place appointed for meeting—Congo Square—and at about half-past eleven o'clock they had all arrived, the majority of them accompanied by field-bands, and with banners and flags floating in the breeze.

In the square a large platform, rising in the form of an amphitheater, had been erected, with a stand for the speakers. The platform was decorated with flags and evergreens, and seats were arranged on and in front of it. The speakers' stand was covered by a large awning, underneath which we found a number of ladies, teachers of the colored schools established by General Banks. Among those present on the platform, we noticed old Jourdan and some fifteen or sixteen of the colored veterans of 1815. Some of them appeared as strong and hearty as the day when they showed their devotion to the glorious stars and stripes.

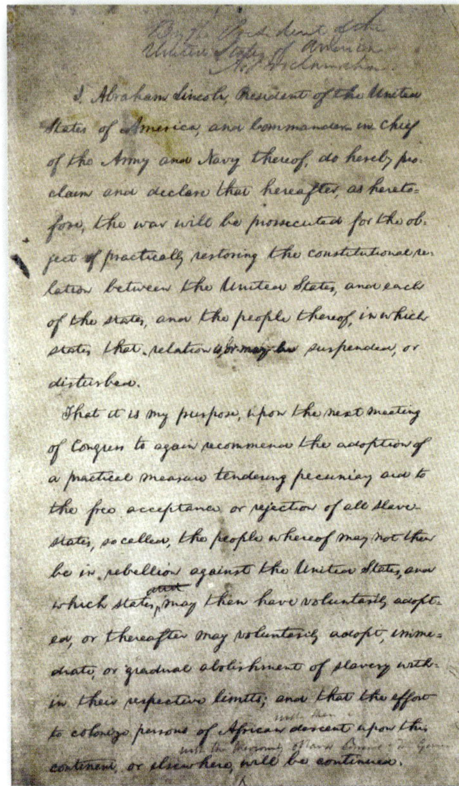

By the President of the United States of America. A Proclamation.

I, Abraham Lincoln, President of the United States of America, and Commander-in-Chief of the Army and Navy thereof, do hereby proclaim and declare that hereafter, as heretofore, the war will be prosecuted for the object of practically restoring the constitutional relation between the United States, and each of the states, and the people thereof, in which states that relation is or may be suspended, or disturbed.

That it is my purpose, upon the next meeting of Congress to again recommend the adoption of a practical measure tendering pecuniary aid to the free acceptance or rejection of all slave-states, so called, the people whereof may not then be in rebellion against the United States, and which states, may then have voluntarily adopted, or thereafter may voluntarily adopt, immediate, or gradual abolishment of slavery within their respective limits; and that the effort to colonize persons of African descent upon this continent, or elsewhere, will be continued.

Top left: "The Emancipation Celebration," *The Era*, June 12, 1864

Top right: Handwritten Emancipation Proclamation by President Lincoln, September 22, 1862.

Effective January 1, 1863, the Emancipation Proclamation freed all enslaved people in Confederate territories that had rebelled against and left the Union—including parts of Louisiana. New Orleans and other locations that the Union had already captured, were not included. The Union, under the leadership of General Benjamin Butler captured New Orleans, the largest confederate city, on May 1, 1862.

After President Lincoln signed the Emancipation Proclamation, the grandest gathering in New Orleans took place in Congo Square. Over 20,000 people joined the parade and festivities. Jordan Noble, the popular drummer, was among the leaders on the podium that day. The following year, an event was held in Congo Square in honor of President Lincoln following his assassination.

Perhaps the most well known events at the location through the years were the Sunday gatherings of enslaved people. Those events made Congo Square a tourist attraction. They also made the location famous around the world.

Names of the Location

Through the years, city records, maps, newspaper articles, and people who visited New Orleans used a variety of names to refer to the location that is now Congo Square. Some were official names that a city ordinance established, but most were popular names that people used over a long period of time. Those names include Place Publique, Place d'Armes, Circus Park, Circus Square, Public Square, Congo green, Congo Park, Place Congo, Congo Plains, Negro Square, the commons, the green expanse, Beauregard Square, and Congo Square.

The name "Congo Square" stood out among the other popular ones. When a city ordinance made Place d'Armes the official name of the location in 1850, newspaper ads included both, Place d'Armes and Congo Square, into the late 1860s.

During the 1880s, the name "Congo Square" gained popularity again and was included on maps and documents of the city. The next official name for the location developed on March 30, 1893, when New Orleans City Council Ordinance 7351 CS changed the popular name of Congo Square to Beauregard Square in honor of Confeder-

Below: "Grand Celebration of the Fourth July," *Daily Picayune*, June 30, 1853. The article shows both names, Place d'Armes and Congo Square

Map of Tremé and Old Basin neighborhood from 1883 with "Congo Square" labeled

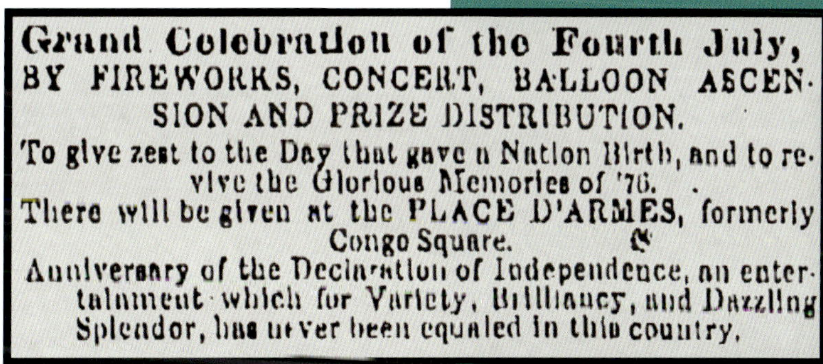

Grand Celebration of the Fourth July, BY FIREWORKS, CONCERT, BALLOON ASCENSION AND PRIZE DISTRIBUTION.
To give zest to the Day that gave a Nation Birth, and to revive the Glorious Memories of '76.
There will be given at the PLACE D'ARMES, formerly Congo Square. &
Anniversary of the Declaration of Independence, an entertainment which for Variety, Brilliancy, and Dazzling Splendor, has never been equaled in this country.

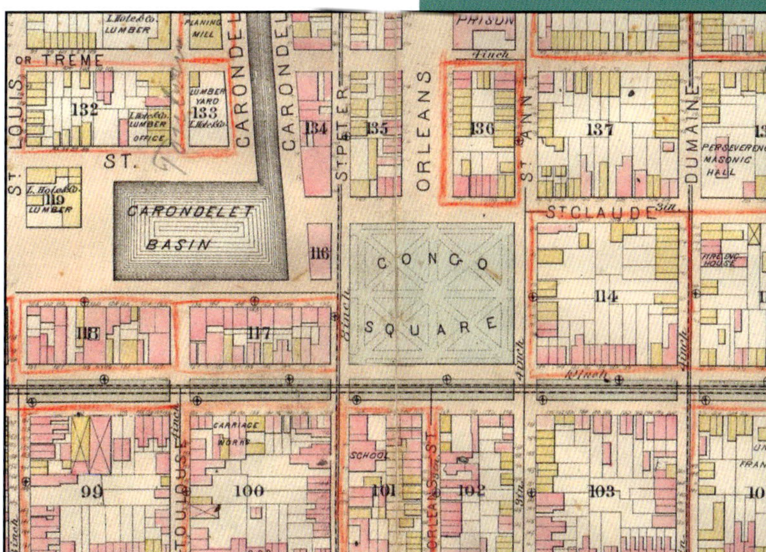

Photograph from 1917 of Congo Square, then "Beauregard Square"

JACKSON
DEMOCRATIC ASSOCIATION,

GRAND
Ratification Meeting
—TO BE HELD AT—
Beauregard Square,
RAMPART AND ORLEANS STREETS,
Tuesday, Oct. 3, 8 P. M.

ate Civil War General P. G. T. Beauregard. People in New Orleans used this name regularly until the late 1970s and 1980s, when there was a surge of interest in the location. The development of Louis Armstrong Park turned attention to Congo Square and its connection to jazz, for which Louis Armstrong gained worldwide fame. In 1993, the Square was listed on the National Register of Historic Places under the name "Congo Square." In 1997, the location received a historic marker with the name "Congo Square." By then, most people in New Orleans didn't realize that the official name was still Beauregard Square.

Daily Picayune, October 2, 1899, naming the location as Beauregard Square

Official Name Change

On April 25, 2011, after receiving a presentation from author and historian Freddi Williams Evans, the New Orleans City Council passed Ordinance Calendar No. 28,411, which made the name of the location "Congo Square." The ordinance, authored by Councilmember Kristin Gisleson Palmer, officially named and dedicated Congo Square in honor of the gatherings of enslaved blacks and free people of color that took place there. Although the popular name for many years had been Congo Square, it had never been official.

At the meeting, author Kalamu ya Salaam talked about the importance of Congo Square to New Orleans, the nation, and the world. Councilmember Palmer then concluded, "By restoring the name, Congo Square will continue to be remembered for the birthplace of the culture and music of New Orleans."

Official Names of Location by Ordinance/Resolution

- Place d'Armes, October 15, 1850
- Beauregard Square, March 30, 1893
- Congo Square, April 25, 2011

View of Congo Square with historical marker in the foreground and the Morris F. X. Jeff Municipal Auditorium in the background. The auditorium, built in 1930, sits on land that once was a part of Congo Square.

The Kongo people were in part identified as speakers of the Kikongo language and as natives of a region in west central Africa known as the Kongo Kingdom. Today, countries that claim parts of that region include the Republic of the Congo, the Democratic Republic of the Congo, Angola, Cabinda, and Gabon.

Why the Name Congo Square?

Two reasons have been found for the popular name Congo Square. During the time of the gatherings, the term "congo" was often used to refer to anything black or anything of African origin. Along those lines, the term "Congo Square" identified the public square for black people. The other reason refers to the people from the Kongo/Angola region of Africa and the Congo, a popular dance that they performed. Research shows that slave traders brought more people from that part of Africa to Louisiana under Spanish and early American rule than from any other region. Some of the dances and music and musical instruments witnessed at the gatherings have been traced to the Democratic Republic of the Congo. When referring to the people from the Kongo/Angola region of Africa, George Washington Cable wrote, "These are they for whom the dance and the place are named."

Circular-designed paving stones on ground of Congo Square completed in 1980 in time for the opening of Louis Armstrong Park

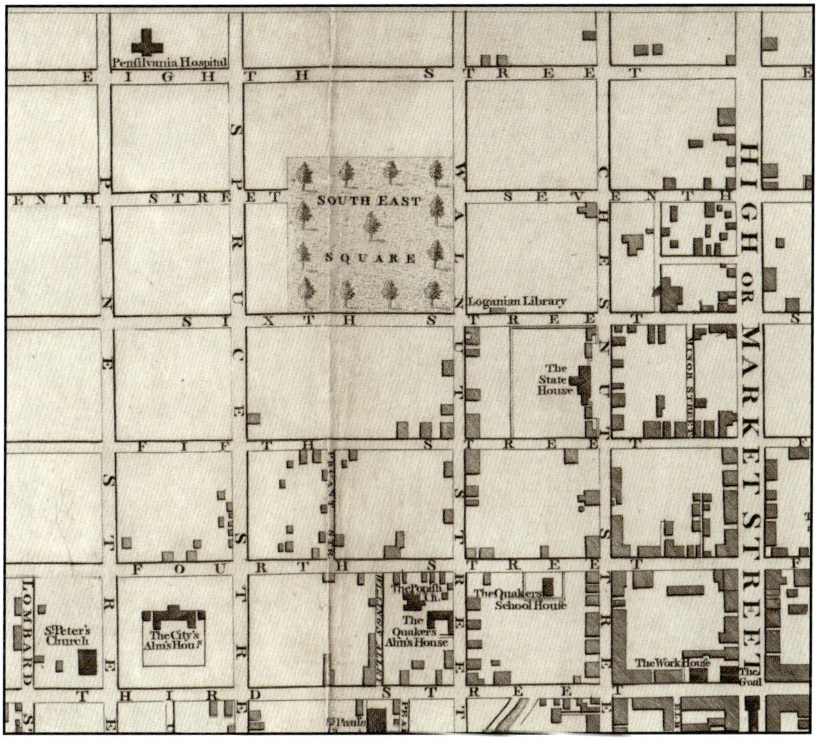

A plan of the city of Philadelphia from 1776. The South East Square was at times used for slave auctions and received the name "Congo Square." Today it is Washington Square.

A New Orleans native, George Washington Cable was an influential author in the late nineteenth century. After fighting for the Confederacy in the Civil War, Cable became a journalist and writer. Many of his fiction and non-fiction works centered on the complex relationships between different races and cultures in New Orleans and the American South. His opposition towards inequality and Jim Crow-era segregation stirred controversy and led him to move to Massachusetts in 1885.

Cable's explanation for the name is the same one given for the name of the location in Philadelphia, Pennsylvania, that was once called Congo Square. Today known as Washington Square, it is situated within the Independence National Historical Park, which includes several sites associated with the American Revolution and the country's founding. The park is called "America's most historic square mile" because of its display of numerous historic landmarks, including Independence Hall, where the Declaration of Independence and United States Constitution were adopted, and the Liberty Bell, one of America's symbols of freedom. The name of Congo Square for that location derived from the Democratic Republic of the Congo in the West Central Region of Africa, where most of the people who gathered there had been born.

2

The People

In order to know who gathered in Congo Square, it is necessary to know which people slave traders brought to Louisiana and which ones remained in New Orleans. The trading of human beings took place under French, Spanish, and American rule, and traders brought people from several regions of West and Central West Africa, various parts of the Caribbean, and many locations within the United States. Those enslaved people, along with some who were born in the Caribbean or America and some who gained their freedom or were born free, made up the black population of the city. People from diverse backgrounds such as those made up the gatherings in Congo Square.

"... My grandmama was stolen from Africa and she lived to be 125 years old. She died last year in April. I think I'll live long as she did. There were fifteen slaves on the land that Duhons had but I never ran round with them. I had room at the back of the big house. You know, Madame Duhon was my grandmamma. She was good to me. The only thing I did was look to my master's horse and be coachman for Madame."

–Victor Duhon, born in Lafayette Parish, Louisiana, was 97 years old when interviewed by the WPA (Works Progress Administration) in the 1930s.

Enslaved Africans

The first two slave ships to arrive in Louisiana, *Aurore* and *Duc du Maine*, came in 1719—bringing in 451 Africans who had survived the journey across the ocean. Around three hundred of them had been born in the Senegambia region of West Africa. Among them were members of the Wolof, Fulbe, Mandinka (Mandingo), Fulani (Fula), and Bambara (Banbara, Bamana, Banmana) nations. Other enslaved Africans brought to Louisiana under the French originated in the Bight of Benin and the West Central region of Africa. They included members of the Nard, Mina, Fon, Yoruba (Nago), Chamba, Ado, and Kongo/Angola nations.

Under Spanish rule, traders brought African captives from the same locations plus the Bight of Biafra. The additional nations included the Caraba, Ibo, Mobo, Kissy, and Canga. People from the West Central region, from the Kongo/Angola nations, were the largest group brought to Loui-

Stowage plan of a British slave ship

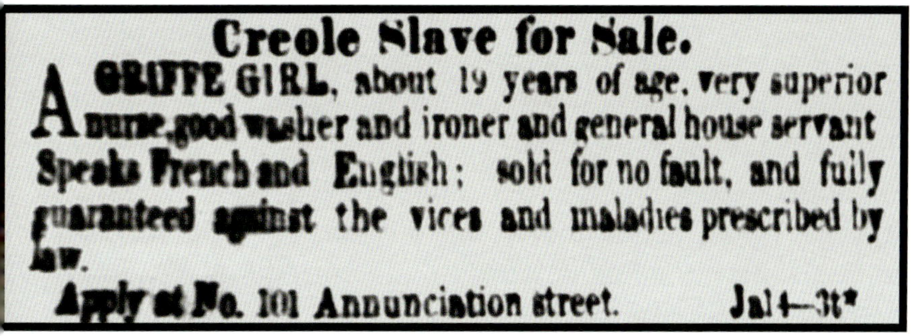

Creole Slave for Sale.

A GRIFFE GIRL, about 19 years of age, very superior nurse, good washer and ironer and general house servant. Speaks French and English; sold for no fault, and fully guaranteed against the vices and maladies prescribed by law.

Apply at No. 101 Annunciation street. Ja14—3t*

"Creole Slave for Sale," *Times Picayune*, January 14, 1857

siana during that period. Children born in Louisiana to these enslaved Africans were sometimes referred to as "Creole slaves." Originally, the term "Creole" identified someone or something (for example, the language, songs, or cooking styles) that began in Louisiana. Enslaved people born in Louisiana often brought higher prices because they spoke the common language, had acquired specific skills, and were already acclimated to the conditions of slavery. Over the years, the term "Creole" took on different meanings to different people.

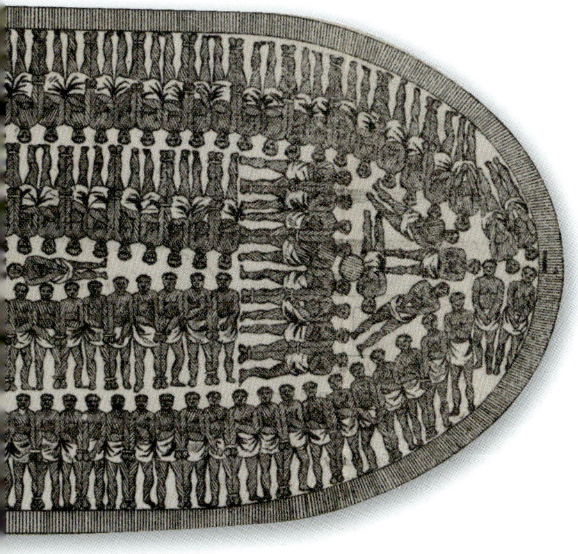

Line of captured people chained together known as a slave coffle

"My grandmudder, she an Africy woman. They brung her freeborn from Africy and some people what knowed things one time tol' us we too proud but us had reason to be proud. My grandmudder's fambly in Africy was a African prince of de rulin' people. My udder grandmudder was a pure bred Indian woman and she raise all my mudder's chillen. My mudder name Eli Chivers."

–Virginia Newman was freeborn, the daughter of a black boat captain and a mother of African and Indian heritage. When a young girl, she apprenticed herself and says she was a nurse girl in the family of Governor Murphy Foster of Louisiana. Ms. Newman was 100 years of age or older when interviewed by the WPA in the 1930s.

From the beginning of American rule in 1803 to the end of the transatlantic slave trade in 1808, the majority of the Africans who slave traders brought to Louisiana were from the West Central region, which included the modern Democratic Republic of the Congo, the Republic of Congo, Angola, Gabon, and other countries. The Africans brought to Louisiana provided labor that built the colony, produced items for exporting, and cultivated food that sustained life. Effective January 1, 1808, the U.S. Congress banned the trade of enslaved people from Africa and other locations outside of this country. After that date, most trading of human beings took place within the United States. Although some traders continued to smuggle enslaved people into the country, the number of enslaved people born in the United States increased, and the number of enslaved people who had been born in Africa decreased. The people, language, music, and dances at the gatherings in Congo Square reflected that change.

Map showing regions in Africa of the transatlantic slave trade

ENSLAVED AND FREE HAITIANS

Haiti became the first black-led republic, but it paid a price for its freedom. France demanded payment in the amount of 150 million francs ($21 billion today) for its loss of enslaved people and its slave colony. Haiti paid off the "independence debt" in 1947, but there has been an outcry for France to repay the money.

Saint-Domingue (now called Haiti) was once the richest territory or colony that France ruled. Since owners did not have to pay enslaved workers, the money earned from large sugar and coffee crops continued to add up. Slave owners became wealthy, and so did the French colony. Rulers in France hoped that Louisiana, the younger French colony, would follow the same footsteps, especially since the two locations had so much in common. Louisiana and Saint-Domingue had the same laws, known as the Code Noir. Both shared the French and Creole languages and the Catholic religion, including the holidays and customs, and both received enslaved people from the same regions in Africa.

That stream of wealth for France would not continue however. Beginning in 1791 and ending in 1804, enslaved people in Saint-Domingue led a successful slave revolt, where they overthrew their owners and won their freedom. The long fight, known as the Haitian Revolution, lasted over twelve years and cost hundreds of thousands of lives. The main leader was Toussaint L'Ouverture, and others included Dutty (Zamba) Boukman, Georges Biassou, Jeannot Bullet, Jean François, Jean-Jacques Dessalines, and Henri Christophe. Some of them lost their lives along the way, but the force of

Depiction of Toussaint L'Ouverture, 1802

Attack and take of the Crête-à-Pierrot in the Haitian Revolution. Original illustration by Auguste Raffet

unity against slavery kept the fight alive. Their victory, the only successful slave revolt in history, shocked the world. It brought freedom to the people and a new name for the country. The name changed from Saint-Domingue to the Republic of Haiti.

Some people who lived there—whites, enslaved people, and free people of color—fled to New Orleans during and following the revolution. This increased the city's population and resulted in more Sunday gatherings as well as more people at the gatherings that already existed. The revolution occurred during Spanish rule in Louisiana, but the Haitians were French speakers and they reinforced the French/Creole language and Catholic-based customs in the city. The black people from Haiti, both enslaved and free, reinforced the African-based music, songs, dances, and religion, specifically Vodou, in New Orleans and particularly at Congo Square.

Vodou is an established religion that developed among enslaved people who combined practices from the Catholic faith with religious practices and beliefs from several African nations.

Enslaved and Free Haitians via Cuba

Although some Haitians fled to New Orleans and other parts of the United States during the revolution, a larger number of them fled to Cuba, which was closer. When war broke out between France and Spain, French refugees, like the Haitians, were forced to leave Cuba and other Spanish colonies. In 1809 thousands of Haitians left Cuba and fled to Louisiana: 3,226 enslaved people, 3,102 free people of color, and 2,731 white people. The majority of them remained in New Orleans, almost doubling the number of people in the city. Once again, they reinforced the French, Creole, and African-based culture that already existed, including the Sunday gatherings at Congo Square.

As a result of the revolution, French planters fled Haiti bringing over 27,000 enslaved people with them. Most of them settled in Cuba's eastern provinces where they introduced sugar cultivation, constructed sugar refineries, and developed coffee plantations. The Haitians brought their culture with them—the music, songs, dances, belief systems, and language. After Spanish, Haitian Creole is the second most-spoken language in Cuba.

Map of the Gulf of Mexico and surrounding countries

"My mother was Della. That was all, jus' Della. My pappy's name was Jim Blair. Both of them was from Virginny, but from diff'rent places, and was brought to Louisiana by . . . traders and sold to Massa Lewis. I know my pappy was lots older than my mother and he had a wife and five children back in Virginny and had been sold away from them out here. Then he and my mother started a family out here. I don't know what become of his family back in Virginny, 'cause when we was freed he stayed with us."

–Virginia Bell was born near Opelousas, Louisiana, and was about 88 years old when interviewed when interviewed by the WPA in the 1930s.

Enslaved Black People born in America

The ban on the transatlantic slave trade, beginning in 1808, increased the domestic slave trade, where black people were bought and sold within the United States. Enslaved black people were sold from states in the upper South including Virginia, Maryland, North Carolina, and Washington, D.C., to states in the lower South including Louisiana. This interstate trade continued for over fifty years. Many of the people involved and who attended the gatherings during that time had been born in the United States, not Africa.

Over 1.2 million people were sold during the domestic trade, and slave traders passed over 100,000 of them through New Orleans. Some came by ship, but many walked the entire distance.

Depiction of enslaved men, women, and children walking past the nation's capitol in Washington, D.C., headed to locations in the lower South during the domestic slave trade

Slave auction in rotunda of the St. Louis Hotel, New Orleans

One of the fears of enslaved people at that time was to be "sold down the river" to New Orleans. As the largest slave-trading center in the country before the Civil War, a person sold from New Orleans could land in any one of the slave-holding states. Sales took place at coffee houses, slave warehouses or pens, city taverns, government buildings, church properties, private residencies, auction houses, public squares, and ballrooms of luxury hotels like the St. Louis Hotel.

A man named Solomon Northup was among those who traders sold in New Orleans during that time. But, unlike most others, he was born free in New York. While traveling and performing as a fiddler in Washington, D.C., Northup was drugged, kidnapped, and shipped to New Orleans where he was sold into slavery. He told about his experiences in his book, *Twelve Years A Slave,* which he wrote after he regained his freedom. Recounts of his story have also been made into a movie. A historic marker now stands at the intersection of Esplanade and Chartres (formerly Moreau) Streets, where he was held in a slave pen until being sold and sent to a Louisiana plantation.

Historic marker for Solomon Northup located at Esplanade and Chartres Street

Published in *Harper's Weekly* in 1873, this illustration by William Ludwell Sheppard, *Negroes Hiding in the Swamps of Louisiana* depicts how some maroons lived. Some also lived in organized communities with enclosed buildings.

Maroons and Runaways

A well-known form of resistance in New Orleans was marronage, where enslaved people escaped to surrounding swamps and lived in organized groups. Legend has it that some maroons returned to the city on Sundays and joined the dances at Congo Square.

The number of maroons grew in New Orleans from a few cases during the French period to several dozens of cases under the Spanish. Juan San Malo (Jean St. Malo in French), was a leader among a network of maroon communities that existed in swamps east of New Orleans near Lake Borgne from around 1780-1784. His camp was called Gaillardeland.

The word maroon derives from the Spanish word "cimarron," which means fugitive.

St. Malo and other maroons, including women and intact families, were known to raid nearby plantations for food and weapons and killed several white people who attempted to re-enslave them or capture them for rewards. Their presence threatened the security of plantation owners who feared that they would incite others to revolt or also runaway.

Repeated attempts by the military, plantation owners, and black spies failed to capture them until 1784 when information about their location led to their arrest. Punishment for the maroons included severe lashings, brandings, and execution by hanging. Juan San Malo was executed on June 19, 1784, in the public square in front of St. Louis Cathedral.

Runaways were people who ran away from their owners hoping to eventually live as free people—whether in New Orleans or far away. The thousands of runaway ads published in New Orleans newspapers give information about those who ran away and about slavery in the city.

Many women who ran away were believed to have remained in the area protected by family and friends. Many of the men who ran away were thought to have hid on ships and sailed up the river. The below runaway ad was for eleven-year-old Lavinia. She had been sold away from her mother to a new owner, who suspected that the mother knew where Lavinia was hiding.

This dirge or funeral song, describing the execution of St. Malo, was first sung in the Creole language and lived in black communities as oral history.

Alas, young men, come make lament, / For poor St. Malo in distress! / They chased, they hunted him with dogs, / They fired a rifle at him. / They dragged him from the cypress swamp. / His arms they tied behind his back. / They tied his hands in front of him. / They tied him to a horse's tail. / They dragged him up into the town. / Before those grand Cabildo men. / They charged that he had made a plot / To cut the throats of all the whites. / They asked him who his comrades were. / Poor St. Malo said not a word! / The judge his sentence read to him. / And then they raised the gallows tree. / They drew the horse—the cart moved off / And left St. Malo hanging there. / The sun was up an hour high / When on the levee he was hung. / They left his body swinging there / For carrion crows to feed upon.

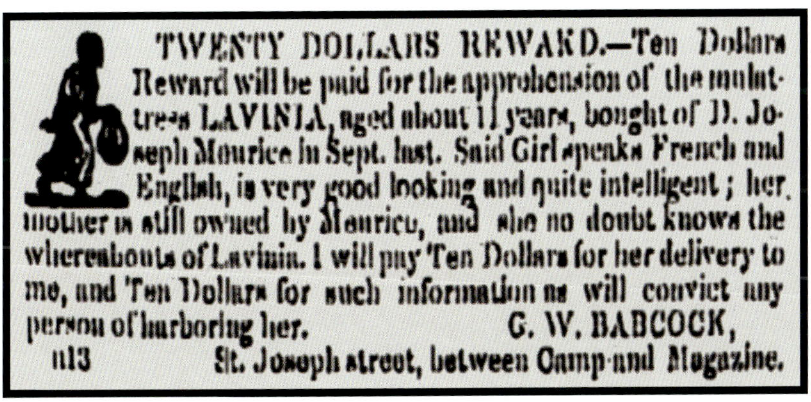
TWENTY DOLLARS REWARD.—Ten Dollars Reward will be paid for the apprehension of the mulatress LAVINIA, aged about 11 years, bought of D. Joseph Maurice in Sept. last. Said Girl speaks French and English, is very good looking and quite intelligent; her mother is still owned by Maurice, and she no doubt knows the whereabouts of Lavinia. I will pay Ten Dollars for her delivery to me, and Ten Dollars for such information as will convict any person of harboring her. G. W. BABCOCK,

n13 St. Joseph street, between Camp and Magazine.

Runaway ad for Lavinia, *Daily Picayune*, November 27, 1849

Bras-Coupé, a fictitious character in George Washington Cable's 1880 novel *The Grandissimes*, was based on a real-life enslaved man named Squire, who ran away from his owner. After several escapes, one of Squire's arms was cut off in 1834 as punishment for his disobedience. However, this did not end his pursuit of freedom as he quickly returned to his life in the swamps outside of New Orleans. Squire boldly re-entered the city often and was reportedly seen participating in the dances at Congo Square several times during this period, an act of defiance that made him a hero among other enslaved people. After several years of escaping capture, and the $2,000 bounty that city officials had placed on his head, Squire was shot and beaten to death by a local fisherman in 1837.

Some of those who ran away managed to reach Ohio or other states where they could live as free people, and perhaps some were successful at living as free in New Orleans. However, many who ran away were captured and returned. Newspapers announced those who had been captured and officials placed them in jails so that owners could retrieve them. Betsy, who ran away with her three children, was not successful. Her owner, Charles Pride, placed a runaway ad in the newspaper beginning in February of 1852 that offered $100 for their return. Two months later, Betsy's husband, a free man of color, was charged and brought to trial for harboring her knowing that she had run away.

ONE HUNDRED DOLLARS REWARD.—Ran away from the subscriber on the 15th inst., a negro woman named BETSY, aged about 35 years, medium size, long nose, pop eyes, upper front teeth out except one; answers quick when spoken to. The above reward will be paid for her apprehension or any information that will lead to it.

The above mentioned woman I will sell running, at a low price, together with her three children.

n16—tf CHAS. PRIDE

Runaway ad for Betsy, *Daily Picayune*, February 20, 1852

HARBORING A SLAVE.—Charles Bell, *alias* Cott, a free man of color, was yesterday brought before Recorder Winter on the charge of having harbored and concealed the slave Betsy, owned by Charles Pride, who ran away about two months ago. Betsy was the wife of Cott; but as it was shown that he had secreted her, knowing that she had run away, he was committed for trial before the First District Court.

Court announcement, "Harboring a Slave," *Daily Picayune*, April 30, 1852

Field Hands and Domestics

Enslaved people who worked in the fields were called field hands, and those who worked inside houses were called domestics, house servants, or house slaves. Some writers reported that those who worked in the fields and on similar jobs came to Congo Square in greater numbers than those who worked as domestics. That was true in part to the fact that there were more field hands than domestic workers.

Most of the people who worked inside houses were women. In addition to cooking and cleaning, many of them cared for young children. In this role, they were called nurses. Writers who witnessed the gatherings reported that some nurses brought the children in their care to Congo Square and stood as spectators.

Top: E. W. Kemble sketch of an enslaved female field hand

Left: The photograph shows men and women working side-by-side cutting sugar cane, c. 1880

After the U.S. Congress abolished the international slave trade in 1808, New Orleans became the center of the domestic slave trade. More than fifty documented sites around the city housed those trades. More enslaved people were sold in New Orleans's slave pens, public squares, government buildings, church properties, city taverns, coffee houses, private residences, auction houses, and even ballrooms of luxury hotels than anywhere else in the United States.

The Hired-Out

Some people whose owners rented or hired them out for different jobs in the city came to Congo Square on Sundays. Although still enslaved, they often lived and worked on their own as if they were free but gave their owners the money that they earned. Laws against enslaved people living away from their owners existed, but the practice continued. The printed advertisement, "New Orleans Slave Depot," offered people for hire by the month.

The hired-out included harness makers, blacksmiths, barbers, carpenters, draymen, market women, hotel waiters, and more. The young boy named Sainville, whose run away ad appears in the Introduction of this book had been hired out for several jobs. He had worked in a cigar factory for two or three years and had sold cakes and beer in the city for a market woman one summer. Sainville was last hired to work at a coal yard. In addition to individual owners, large corporations such as the city of New Orleans, the New Orleans Gas Company, the Pontchartrain and New Orleans Railroad Company, and the Red Brick and Tile Company hired-out or rented the labor of skilled and unskilled enslaved people.

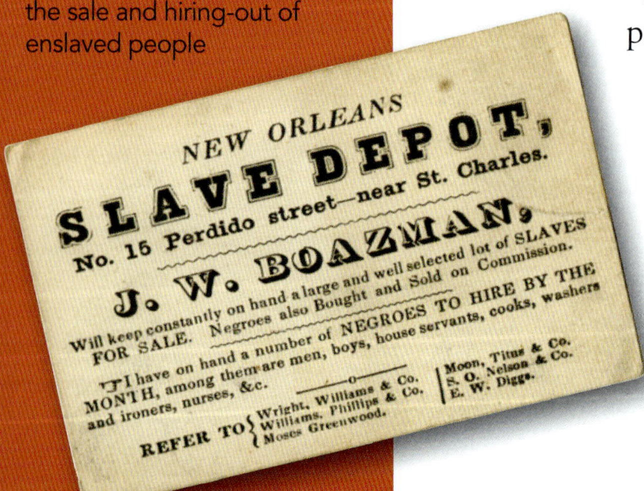
NEW ORLEANS
SLAVE DEPOT,
No. 15 Perdido street—near St. Charles.
J. W. BOAZMAN,
Will keep constantly on hand a large and well selected lot of SLAVES FOR SALE. Negroes also Bought and Sold on Commission.
☞ I have on hand a number of NEGROES TO HIRE BY THE MONTH, among them are men, boys, house servants, cooks, washers and ironers, nurses, &c.
REFER TO { Wright, Williams & Co. | Williams, Phillips & Co. | Moses Greenwood. | Moon, Titus & Co. | S. O. Nelson & Co. | E. W. Diggs.

New Orleans Slave Depot printed card advertising the sale and hiring-out of enslaved people

Slave traders or trading firms kept "slave depots," also called "slave pens" and "slave yards" such as the "New Orleans Slave Depot" and the pen located at 156 Commons Street, where they held enslaved people until they were taken to auction, hired out, or sold at the site. The locations often held fifty to one hundred people crowded together in horrible conditions before they were carried to one of the markets such as the St. Louis Hotel, the St. Charles Hotel, or the exchange on Esplanade Avenue.

A SLAVE-PEN AT NEW ORLEANS—BEFORE THE AUCTION. A SKETCH OF THE PAST.

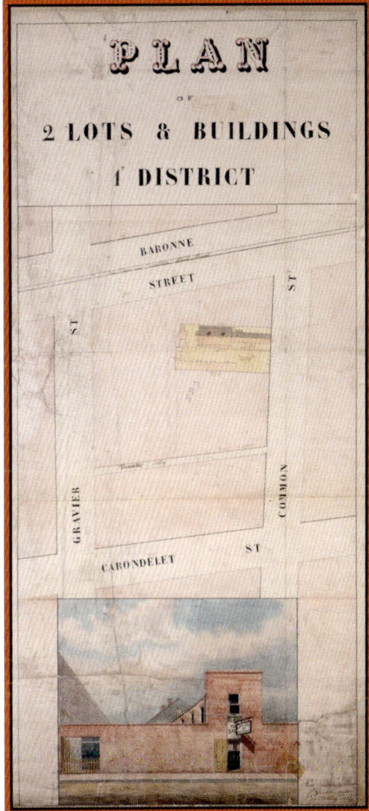

Right: Building at 156 Commons Street, referred to as a "slave pen" or "slave yard" where enslaved people were held until sold. Above and below images depict enslaved people dressed for auctions.

Traders prepared enslaved people for those markets to increase prices and speed up sales. For men, beards were shaved, hair was combed, and gray hairs plucked or blackened with dye. Men and women were often dressed in new clothing. Women were given long-sleeved dresses with aprons and kerchiefs to cover their heads. Men were often given black suits with top hats, as seen in the doorway of the illustration that depicts a scene at 156 Commons Street.

Skilled Laborers

"The survival of French Louisiana was due not only to African labor but also to African technology. The introduction from Africa of rice seed and of slaves who knew how to cultivate rice assured the only reliable food crop that could be grown in the swamplands in and around New Orleans."

–from *Africans in Colonial Louisiana* by Gwendolyn Midlo Hall

As noted, many of the people who were hired-out had special work skills. Some had learned those skills in New Orleans. Some had gained them in other parts of the state or country, and some brought skills with them from Africa or parts of the Caribbean. In all cases, those with special skills brought more money, and slave traders sought after them.

The captains of the first slave ships that landed in Louisiana were instructed to purchase Africans with certain skills. John Law, who headed the Company of the Indies and managed the growth and development of the colony in the early 1700s, ordered the captains to also buy three to four barrels of rice for seeding and Africans who knew how to cultivate it. Rice became an important food item for the early colony and a main food item in Louisiana-style dishes called Creole cooking. Rice grew so well that the colony made money by exporting it to other locations.

Slave traders brought Africans from the Senegambia region who knew how to process indigo plants, and indigo, which was used to make a dark-blue dye, also became an exported product that made money for Louisiana. During the French period, slave traders brought cane seed and enslaved men who knew how to grow sugar cane to Louisiana

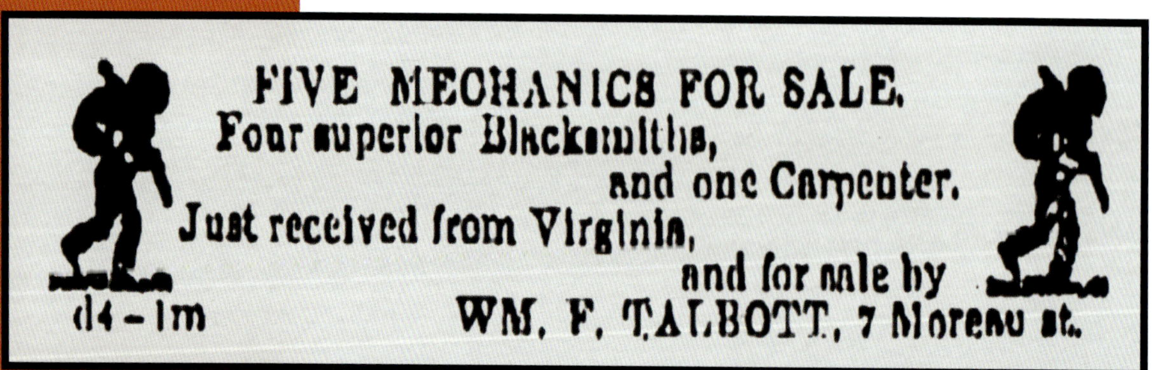

"Five Mechanics for Sale," *Daily Picayune*, December 24, 1852

from the West Indies. The interest in sugar cane grew after the Haitian Revolution with the migration of sugar planters to Louisiana. Business grew and sugar became a major product that planters sold to other locations.

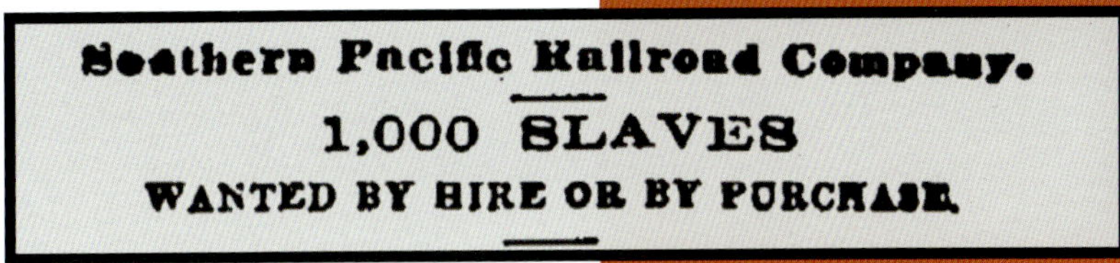

Southern Pacific Railroad Company.

1,000 SLAVES

WANTED BY HIRE OR BY PURCHASE.

Southern Pacific Railroad Wanted Advertisement for enslaved people, *Daily Picayune*, May 19, 1861

Africans possessed other skills when they landed in Louisiana. Some were cooks, language interpreters, lumberjacks, healers, navigators, sail makers, ship builders, silver and goldsmiths, merchants, metal workers, wet nurses, basket weavers, leather workers, cloth weavers, and horse trainers. Some had herded cattle, built dwellings, and made clothing. The skills that each enslaved person possessed or the work category in which he/she had been placed was advertised at the time of sale. Newspaper articles and other advertisements listed them. Some ads used the term "mechanics" to identify carpenters, blacksmiths, and those with related skills.

Enslaved people brought more than physical labor. They introduced new foodways including one-pot dishes such as stews and gumbos. Some words, including "gumbo" also came with them. They brought food items including okra, black-eyed peas, and watermelon, and they brought their culture—their music, dances, songs, religions, and marketing traditions. At every opportunity, they came together to keep their culture alive. They did so despite the conditions of slavery that sold family members away from each other and laws that intended to make them forget or deny their heritage. Such laws included the Code Noir, which directed owners to baptize all enslaved people in the Catholic faith. The opportunity to perpetuate African cultural practices on Sunday afternoons made Congo Square a place of resistance as well as a place of celebration.

James Derham, born enslaved, is generally recognized as the first African American physician in the United States. Derham accompanied his owner, a doctor, to the battlefield during the American Revolution, where he provided menial medical services to British troops. Derham was sold to a doctor in New Orleans and purchased his freedom there in 1783, whereupon he established his own medical practice treating white and black patients. Dr. Benjamin Rush, a signer of the Declaration of Independence, read a paper authored by Derham before the College of Physicians of Philadelphia in 1888. Derham continued to practice medicine in New Orleans until just before the Louisiana Purchase when Spanish officials tightened regulations requiring doctors to have accredited medical degrees.

Under French rule, there were less than 100 free people of color in the colony. Under the Spanish, the number grew to approximately 1,500 because of new laws and increased opportunities for enslaved people to purchase their freedom.

Free People of Color

Black people who had gained their freedom or were born free were called "free people of color" or *gens de couleur libres*. They had received their freedom in one of three ways:

1) If their mother was free, they would have been born free.

2) They may have earned enough money on their time off to buy their freedom from the person who owned them.

3) They may have been set free, or emancipated, by their previous owner.

The third scenario is demonstrated in this letter that Philip Moore presented to the court in 1847. It stated that his mother, on her deathbed, wished to set an enslaved female named Henrietta free. No age was given for Henrietta, but she was an adult. As in this case, enslaved women were called girls regardless of their age. Henrietta worked as a washerwoman. The letter also stated that for the previous six years, her owner had allowed her to work and make her own living away from the owner's control.

A young free woman of color, known as "Betsy," wearing a yellow tignon

The letter reads:

To the Honorable, the Recorder &
Council of Municipality No Two
Respectfully represents
Philip Moore, of New Orleans -

That it was the dying wish of his late mother and so expressed in her last will, that her slave girl "Henrietta" should be emancipated.

That your Petitioner, as executor of the said will, was charged with this duty -

That the said girl Henrietta has now reached the age requisite by law to be attained before emancipation is allowed -

That from a tender age she has lived in New Orleans, always in the Second Municipality & has never been in a state where slavery is prohibited -

That for the last six years she has been allowed to gain her own livelihood, away from her Petitioners control, & has habit of labor & thrift & her uniform good conduct agrees your petitioner that she is well worthy of freedom & will not abuse it's [*sic*] exercise.

Your petitioner is read to give the security required by law for the emancipation of said slave. In good condition for her good conduct while she remains in the state -

That is the desire of said Henrietta to remain in the state & and leave [live] to this is prayed for - Wile it please your Hon. Body to make the necessary orders herein, to the - the prayer of your Petitioner be granted -

Witness
Wheelock S. Upton

Philip Moore Executor

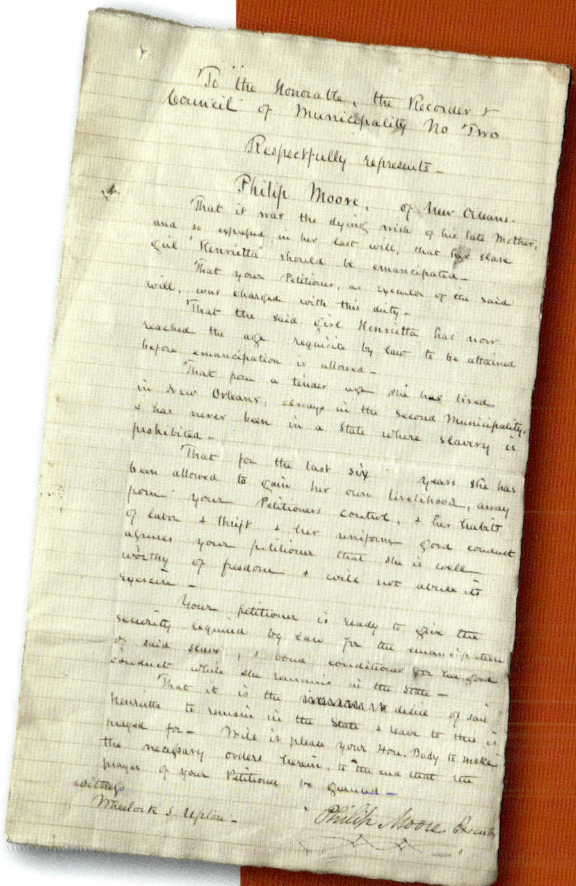

Letter of emancipation for Henrietta

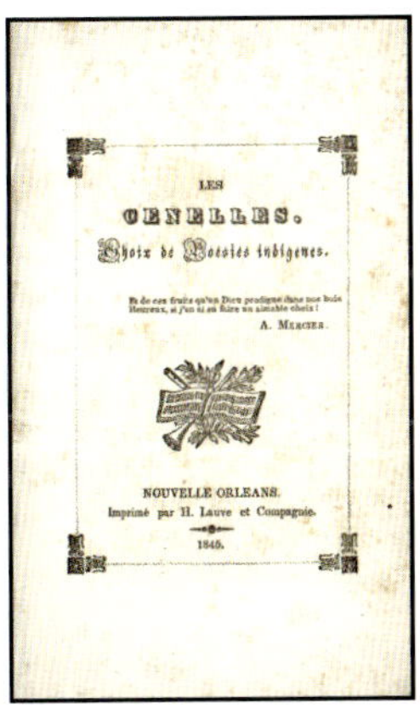

Published in 1845 in New Orleans, *Les Cenelles* was the first collection of poems by people of African heritage in the United States.

As a result of the Haitian Revolution, many free people of color from Haiti migrated to Louisiana, which augmented the number of free persons of color in the colony. Those Haitians, as well as ones who were enslaved, greatly impacted New Orleans culture, including the architecture, cuisine, literature, music, and dance.

As an enslaved woman, Henrietta would have wrapped her head with a handkerchief or piece of fabric because it was the custom to do so. As a free woman of color (FWC), she would have wrapped her head because an ordinance or law required her to do so. The ordinance, passed in 1786, stated that free women of color could not wear their hair high on their heads in fancy styles with feathers or curls. They had to wear their hair flat or wrap their heads with a handkerchief known as a tignon. This kept free women of color connected to enslaved women who also kept their heads wrapped.

The portraits below show free women of color wearing tignons or head wraps. They generally used more fabric for their tignons and created tall and fancy designs. Although many free people of color had white fathers or grandfathers and therefore had fair skin tones, some free people of color had brown skin tones. While many free people of color attended their own dances and were able to gather or visit other places on Sundays, some of them chose to join the gatherings in Congo Square.

Bottom left: Painting of an unidentified woman wearing a tignon

Bottom right: Painting of Mrs. Juliet Noel (Pierre) Toussaint, FWC, by Anthony Meucci, 1825

CONGO SQUARE.—This well known place of resort for the colored people of our city, presents a most animated appearance on Sundays and holidays. Yesterday the square was thronged with the *habitués* of the region scattered about in groups, dancing, singing and laughing to the tuneless accompaniments of squeaking fiddles, antiquated tambourines and attenuated banjos. The sky was clear and bright, the grass dry, the air mild and balmy, and the way the "colored folks" did heel and toe it was a persimmon above the most strenuous efforts of Daddy Rice. Congo Square is well worth a visit from the stranger or any one else who desires to be amused by the peculiarities of the negro race.

"Congo Square," *Daily Picayune*, December 22, 1848

SPECTATORS

Newspaper articles like the one above and travelers who wrote about the gatherings encouraged people to visit Congo Square. James Creecy, who traveled to the city in the 1830s, wrote that every stranger should visit Congo Square at least once. No one would regret or forget it. People who lived in New Orleans as well as travelers came to see the dancers. However, some spectators, such as circus producers and minstrel show performers did not come for entertainment only. Edwin Pierce (E. P.) Christy of the world-famous troupe Christy Minstrels, who lived in the city for a period of time, stated that he received material for his shows from Congo Green, another name used for Congo Square.

View of Congo Square by George Mungier, c. 1890-95

3

An Urban Slave Society

The location of New Orleans on the Mississippi River made the city one of the most popular ports in the South for trading goods and led to the name "Queen City on the River." This economic exchange included the long-time and large-scale trade of human beings. Despite New Orleans's role as the largest port during the domestic slave trade, the city had one of the largest numbers of free people of color in the country. It also had a significant number of enslaved people who were hired-out and who lived as if they were free. In New Orleans, enslaved people were able to gather by the hundreds in public places with people from other parts of the city who had different owners and with black people who were free. Some family members belonged to different owners within the city, some families included both free and enslaved people, and there were some marriages between free and enslaved people.

A picayune was a Spanish coin that was small in size and worth very little.

One of the places where everyone could come together in the open was Congo Square on Sunday afternoons. An 1864 newspaper article stated that it was a place for people to meet old loved ones, make new friends, talk over past affairs, make new plans, and "spend whatever surplus picayunes and dimes they may have acquired from their honest labors, or which came to them either as incentives or rewards for good conduct." Gatherings continued there off and on into the 1850s. Enslaved people gathered at Congo Square longer than at any other public place in North America. A combination of factors created the social, political, and economic system of New Orleans through which tens of thousands of enslaved people navigated for nearly 150 years.

The Laws

Enslaved people in New Orleans were allowed to congregate on Sunday afternoons for social and recreational purposes under the French beginning in 1718, the Spanish beginning officially in 1763, and the Americans beginning in 1803. Under French rule, the law of the land was the Code Noir or Black Code, which the king of France, Louis XIV, passed in 1685 to define the conditions of slavery for all territories owned by France including Louisiana and Saint-Domingue. Louisiana adopted the Code Noir in 1724. These are four of the fifty-five articles that it included.

- No Jews could live in the colony.
- Slaves had to be baptized in the Roman Catholic faith.
- Only the Roman Catholic religion was allowed in the colony.
- Sundays and holidays had to be observed. All negroes found working on those days were to be taken from their owners.

Spanish Govenor Francisco Luis Héctor de Carondelet issued decrees or regulations for those enslaved, which established monthly food rations; gave them Sundays off unless paid; prohibited them from working before daybreak and after sunset; limited lashes received to 30 within 24 hours; and fined owners who did not adhere.

Code Noir (Black Code), adopted in 1724

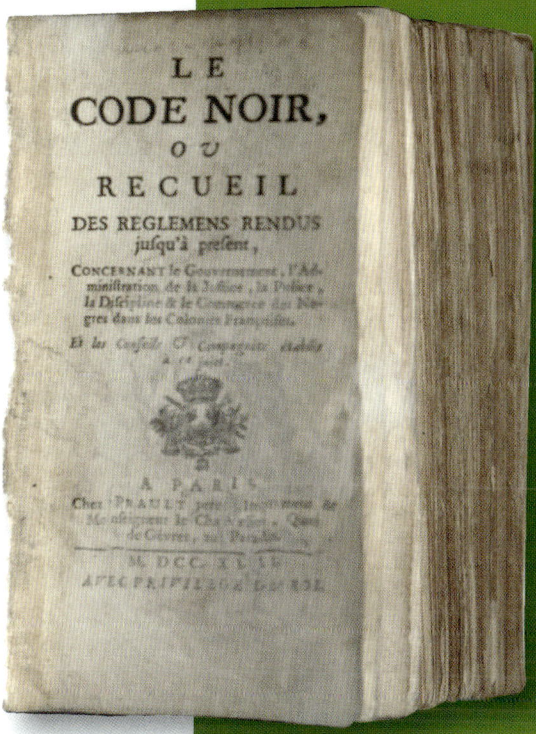

Article V. declared that Sundays were holy days and must be work-free for everyone in the colony, which included enslaved people. As a result, some of them received money from their owners when they worked on Sundays, and some earned money by working for other people, with their owner's permission. If time and owners allowed, some enslaved people earned money by selling items that they made, such as pralines and pies; that they grew in their garden plots, such as vegetables; that they hunted, such as rabbits; and that they gathered from nature, such as wild berries and moss from trees. Over time, some enslaved people earned and saved enough money to buy their freedom. Others earned and saved enough money to buy clothing, shoes, and enough food to eat.

The Sisters of the Holy Family is an African American female religious order established in New Orleans by Henriette DeLille, a free woman of color, in 1837. These Roman Catholic nuns provided nursing care for the elderly, operated a home for orphans, and established schools that taught children who were enslaved at a time when such education was prohibited by law.

Sisters of the Holy Family in New Orleans, c. 1899

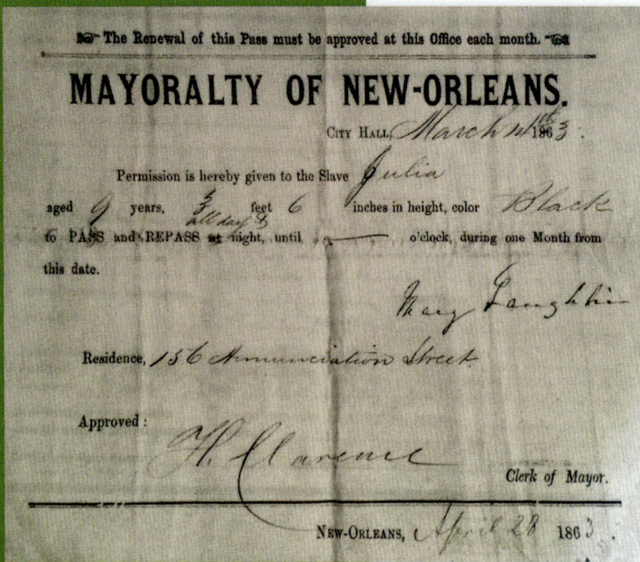

The Renewal of this Pass must be approved at this Office each month.

MAYORALTY OF NEW-ORLEANS.

City Hall, March 14th 1863.

Permission is hereby given to the Slave Julia aged 9 years, 3 feet 6 inches in height, color Black to PASS and REPASS all day & night, until — o'clock, during one Month from this date.

Mary Laughlin

Residence, 156 Annunciation Street

Approved: H. Clarence Clerk of Mayor.

New-Orleans, April 28 1863.

Pass for Julia, an enslaved girl, nine years old

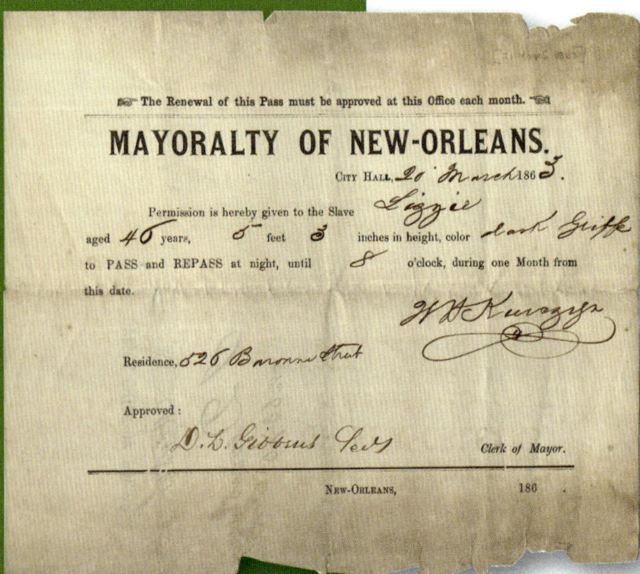

The Renewal of this Pass must be approved at this Office each month.

MAYORALTY OF NEW-ORLEANS.

City Hall, 20 March 1863.

Permission is hereby given to the Slave Lizzie aged 46 years, 5 feet 3 inches in height, color dark Griff to PASS and REPASS at night, until 8 o'clock, during one Month from this date.

W H Kursziger

Residence, 526 Baronne Street

Approved: D. L. Gibbons Secy Clerk of Mayor.

New-Orleans, 186 .

Pass for Lizzie, an enslaved woman

Although the Code Noir did not give them the right to do so, enslaved people came together on Sunday afternoons to enjoy themselves. They gathered on the west bank of the river, along the levee, in back yards, and in public squares including the main square—present-day Jackson Square.

Similar conditions for Sundays existed under Spanish and American rule. Laws during those eras included the Carondelet Decrees of 1795 under the Spanish and the Black Codes of 1806 under the Americans. At no time, however, were enslaved people able to gather without permission. The gatherings ended at sunset, and everyone had to be back where they resided by nine o'clock or face jail time and/or receive lashes with a whip. To signal the curfew, officials fired a cannon that was located in Jackson Square, until 1850 when it was moved to Congo Square.

When walking from place to place in the city, enslaved people often carried passes like the examples shown here. The first pass was issued to a forty-six-year-old woman named Lizzie on March 20, 1863. It was good for one month ending at eight o'clock each night. Nine-year-old Julia and other children also received passes to move around the city and work. The runaway ad for

Pelagie and her son, Pierre, tells that they both had passes, such as the examples shown here, when they ran away. The owner had given passes to them to move around the city and hire themselves for different jobs. Pierre found work in various cotton presses in the city.

A law or city ordinance in 1817 called for the mayor to appoint places for enslaved people to gather. Although no documentation of his appointments have been found, Congo Square became the only place where such events were held. It remained the official gathering place until the Sunday gatherings were no longer permitted. An 1857 city council ordinance allowed enslaved people to assemble on the grounds for the purpose of dancing or playing ball or cricket with permission from the mayor that specified that day only and ending at sunset. It appears that this was the last ordinance that would have given enslaved people that permission.

The Ordinances of 1811 forbade enslaved people to assemble except for pre-approved funerals, dances, or sports, and restricted their meetings for recreational purposes to Sunday, until sundown, at places designated by the mayor.

$20 REWARD.

Ran away from their mistress, Madame Marguerette Jardell alias Maxuur, the negress PELAGIE and The mulatto PIERRE, her son. The negress is supposed to be in the lower part of the city concealed by some white person. The mulatto Pierre has been in the habit of being employed about the different cotton presses in this city. Each of said slaves had a pass to hire themselves during the month of February. The above reward will be given to any person who will confine the said slaves in the parish prison, or deliver them into the charge of the subscriber.

mar 5 3t O. B. HILL, 33 Camp street.

Runaway ad for Pelagie and Pierre, *Daily Picayune*, March 5, 1841

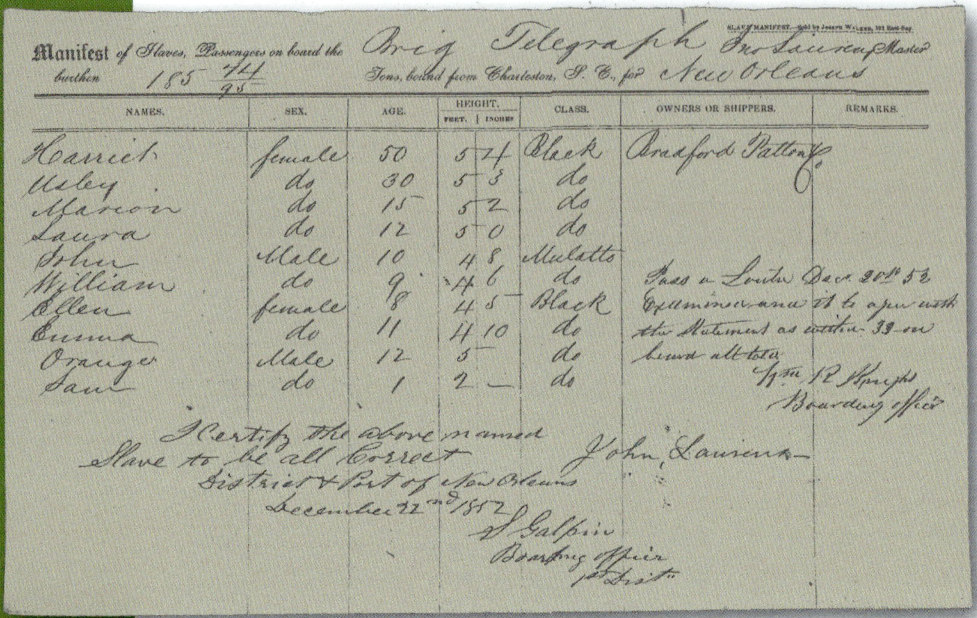

Manifest of Slaves, Passengers on board the Brig Telegraph Jno Laurens Master burthen 185 74/95 Tons, bound from Charleston, S. C., for New Orleans

NAMES.	SEX.	AGE.	HEIGHT. FEET.	HEIGHT. INCHES	CLASS.	OWNERS OR SHIPPERS.	REMARKS.
Harriet	female	50	5	4	Black	Bradford Patton & Co	
Usley	do	30	5	3	do		
Marion	do	15	5	2	do		
Laura	do	12	5	0	do		
John	Male	10	4	8	Mulatto		
William	do	9	4	6	do		
Ellen	female	8	4	5	Black		
Emma	do	11	4	10	do		
Orange	Male	12	5		do		
Sam	do	1	2		do		

I Certify the above named Slave to be all Correct John Laurens

District & Port of New Orleans December 22nd 1852

S Galpin Boarding officer 1st Dist

Ship manifest or cargo document for the *Brig Telegraph* with a list of cargo, which included ten enslaved Africans who disembarked in New Orleans

A Port City

As a port, various kinds and sizes of ships and boats lined loading docks up and down the Mississippi riverfront. Such vessels transported products, people, and culture in and out of New Orleans. In 1835, the Port of New Orleans achieved $54 million in business. By 1840, some four hundred steamboats traveled the river engaging in one form of business or another. That same year, the Port of New Orleans was considered to be the fourth busiest port in the world, and it played a major role in the shipping of enslaved people during that time. The port's impact on the slave trade can be seen through ship manifests or ship records, slave sales, runaway ads, and other sources including songs that gatherers sang at Congo Square and elsewhere. The songs "Carry Me Back to Old Virginia," and "Virginia Never Tire" were popular during the years of the domestic slave trade.

In 1808, the United States banned the international slave trade, though illegal shipments of Africans to Louisiana continued, with the last documented slave ship, the *Fenix*, arriving in New Orleans in 1830.

Above: Barrels of sugar crowd New Orleans's Sugar Levee in 1902

Left: *Giant Steamboats at New Orleans*, 1853, by Hippolyte Sebron shows steamboats *Gipsy*, *Grand Turk*, and others at the Sugar Levee and a wharf busy with stevedores.

Parlange Plantation "big house" in New Roads, Louisiana

Plantations along the Mississippi River and German Coast area provided much of the food for New Orleans. It was the cultivation of cash crops such as indigo, cotton, and sugar, however, that increased the demand for enslaved men and women in Louisiana in the late eighteenth and early nineteenth centuries.

Urban vs Rural Slavery

Life for enslaved people in cities or urban areas, like New Orleans, was quite different from life on rural plantations. In contrast to the hundreds of acres of land on most rural plantations, the smaller house plots in the city made enslaved people and their owners live closer together. In cities, enslaved people sometimes slept in attics, back rooms, or a building very close by. On plantations, houses for the enslaved, called slave quarters, were a distance away from the "big house," or place where the owners lived.

In cities, enslaved people worked a wider variety of jobs. Women who worked as domestics shopped for the food at markets, cooked for and served households, washed, ironed, took care of children, and cleaned homes, hotels, restaurants, cotton presses, and other businesses. Some of them ran their own businesses as washerwomen, cooks, and *marchandes*, or market women, selling food in market places. In those cases, they gave their owners the money that they earned. Although many of those jobs existed in rural ar-

Rural slave quarters at Magnolia Plantation in Natchitoches, Louisiana

Below: Slave quarters in the New Orleans French Quarter with standard slanted roof that faced inward towards the often-small courtyard that separated the quarters from the owner's residence

eas, there were fewer of them, which pushed most women into the fields to work alongside men.

For enslaved men, New Orleans offered highly skilled jobs as engineers, bricklayers, cobblers, harness makers, hotel and restaurant waiters, and blacksmiths, among others. In many cases, these skilled workers were rented or hired-out and sometimes lived away from their owners. In New Orleans, enslaved men also worked in shipyards, brickyards, cotton presses, and warehouses. Again, such jobs were few or did not exist in rural areas, which pushed most men into the fields to work as field hands.

In New Orleans, enslaved people mingled with people who were free, those who were hired-out and lived as if they were free, and those who belonged to other owners. It was easier in the city than in rural areas to form and join groups for various purposes. It was also easier to blend in and remain unnoticed, particularly for those who ran away from their owners.

Between 1719 and 1808, around 12,000 captured Africans were taken from their homelands and brought to Louisiana. The average time between a ship's departure from Africa and its arrival in Louisiana was 61.7 days. Of the nearly 12,000 Africans who were boarded onto ships bound for Louisiana, around 10,000 of them survived the journey and were sold into slavery.

Resistance

The runaway ads that appear in this book represent one of the numerous ways enslaved people fought against slavery. For many, efforts to resist the inhumane and often brutal system began the moment they were captured in their homelands. Some refused to eat and others attempted suicide in holding pens along the coast of Africa as they awaited ships of departure. During the treacherous journey across the Atlantic Ocean, known as the Middle Passage, some jumped overboard and some rose up against their capturers. Many women who were expecting babies opted to end the lives of their unborn or newborns to prevent them from a life of slavery. This also deprived their owners of additional labor that would bring a profit.

The thousands of runaway ads published in New Orleans newspapers tell of forged passes, false emancipation papers, physical disguises, assistance from friends and relatives, and theft of property and money. Some owners suspected that those who ran away, particularly women, were still in the city hiding among family and friends. Sometimes those family members were free people of color.

Right: An example of the icon that identifies a runaway advertisement

In the announcement below, Charlotte, who ran away, was married to a free man, and her owner suspected that her husband was hiding her. In the next announcement, Caroline, who ran away, had a sister and mother, who were both free and who lived on Orleans Street near the parish prison. Orleans Street bordered Congo Square and the prison was behind the Square. The owner also stated in the ad that Caroline was fond of dancing at balls. Those balls may

$25 REWARD,

Will be paid for the delivery, in any of the prisons of the city or state, of a Creole negresse named CHARLOTTE, about 34 years of age, who has now been absent more than three months. She is black, with rather red eyes, full round face, of good countenance, is well made, and speaks French and a little English. She has a free colored man for husband, and is no doubt harbored by him. An additional sum of $25 will be paid to any one who will give such information as will lead to the detection of the person harboring her.

A short time since a person called, in my absence, to say that he had seen the above slave, but refusing to leave his name, I have not since heard from him; but should this meet his eye, he is requested to call again. [may 31 3t] N. N. WILKINSON.

Runaway ad for Charlotte
Daily Picayune, June 2, 1840

have been the dances at Congo Square as they were sometimes referred to as balls. The balls may have also been the dances given for free people of color, and Caroline may have attended them with her mother and sister. Actually, she probably attended both kinds of events. The long-term observance of African-based music, dance, marketing, and religion made the gatherings themselves a form of resistance.

Council member Wiltz, with permission of the council, presented a resolution "authorizing free Negroes and slaves to give balls on Circus Square (Congo Square) from 12'o clock until sunset under surveillance of the police."

–First Municipal Council Ordinances & Resolutions, August 28, 1837

TWENTY-FIVE DOLLARS REWARD will be paid for the apprehension and lodgement in any of the jails of the city of the mulatress CAROLINE, who belonged a few months ago to Widow D. Bouligny. Her mother, named Cornlie, and her sister Pauline, both free, reside in Orleans street, near the parish prison Caroline is twenty-eight years old, and her hair is cropped close. She is frequently disorderly, and is very fond of dancing at balls. She ran away on the morning of the 27th of April.
ap28 6t* OR. HARAN.

Runaway ad for Caroline
Daily Picayune, May 5, 1849

Less obvious and often unreported forms of resistance included work slow downs, broken tools and machinery, faked illnesses, arson, and contaminated food for owners. The most well known group efforts in Louisiana were slave revolts that occurred in Pointe Coupée Parish in 1795, St. Martin Parish in 1840, and along the German Coast in 1811. Historians regard the 1811 revolt as the largest slave uprising in U.S. history. Marronage, another form of group opposition to slavery, was common in the New Orleans area as seen in Chapter 2.

Every act of resistance, large or small, individual or group, carried the risk of severe punishment if uncovered. Runaway ads attest to the cutting off of body parts (i.e. ears, toes, feet), branding with hot irons, and severe lashings called flogging. In New Orleans, officials detained or placed captured runaways in jails and announced their whereabouts in newspaper ads so owners could retrieve their "property," as enslaved people were regarded. In the meantime, officials placed captured runaways in chains and

BROUGHT to the Second Municipality Police Prison—
THOMAS, a dark griff, aged 27 years, 5 feet 7 inches high; says he belongs to Mr. McMullen, of Mobile, Ala.
MALEY, a dark griffe, aged about 51 years, 4 feet 11 inches high; says she belongs to Mme. Fryer, of New Orleans.
SARAH, a griffe, aged about 29 years, 4 feet 10 inches high; says she belongs to Mr. Jolie, of NewOrleans.
KEZIAH, a dark griffe, aged about 55 years, cross eyed, is 5 feet 3 inches high; says she belongs to Mr. Pinta, of New Orleans.
The owners will please comply with the law and take them away. J. WORRELL, Warden.
New Orleans, December 4, 1851. d5 1aw3w

Daily Crescent, December 4, 1851

On the night of January 8, 1811, Charles Deslondes and a group of other enslaved people located along the German Coast, about thirty miles upriver from New Orleans, set in motion a well-calculated uprising and began marching toward New Orleans. As they proceeded down the River Road toward the city, their numbers grew. Approximately 500 people eventually joined the rebellion, making it the largest slave uprising in American history. On January 10, several militia groups and regular U.S. Army troops overtook them. Armed with nothing more than simple farm equipment, they were no match for the military forces, and some were killed immediately. A quickly arranged trial convicted those who survived, and punishment, including executions, was ordered. Reportedly, one of the conspirators, a lieutenant named Gilbert, was hung in Congo Square.

Vue d'une Rue du Faubourg Ste. Marie, Nelle Orleans depicts a gang of enslaved people working on the streets of New Orleans. The men's legs are shackled in chains while the woman wears an iron collar, likely in punishment for attempting to run away.

assigned them to public work details as depicted in the lithograph *Vue d'une Rue du Faubourg Ste. Marie, Nelle Orleans,* (1821) by Felix Achille de Beaupoil, Marquis de Saint-Aulaire.

Once back with their owners, additional punishment ensued, as was the case of Wilson Chinn, the man in this photograph who was branded by his owner. Chinn was among eight enslaved people who General Butler emancipated when he occupied New Orleans at the beginning of the Civil War. Colonel George Hanks brought the group to New York, where they were photographed. Chinn appears in several photographs taken during that time including the one here entitled "Learning is Wealth."

Wilson, Charley, Rebecca, and Rosa were former slaves emancipated and brought to New York

4

The Gatherings

The privilege for enslaved people to gather on Sunday afternoons was always under threat of being taken away, and it often was. Any attempt or rumor of an attempt to gain freedom, such as a slave plot or slave revolt, led city officials to stop the events or add tighter controls. For example, city officials tightened controls after the 1811 slave revolt during which over five hundred people rose up against their owners. The revolt began up the river from New Orleans in St. John the Baptist Parish. It was the largest slave revolt in United States history. Within a week after the revolt ended, the New Orleans City Council passed a law that banned enslaved people from sleeping in any house other than that of their owners, renting a house, gathering for any meeting that was not pre-approved, and only gathering for recreation on Sundays until sundown at places set by the mayor.

In that case, Sunday gatherings continued in New Orleans, but officials in some other parts of the state banned them altogether. In cases where officials in New Orleans banned the gatherings, in time, new leaders and new ordinances usually reinstated them. The following ordinance restored the gatherings in 1845 after they had ceased for a while. The name of the location was then called "Circus Place" (place du Cirque). The newspaper article published two months after officials passed the ordinance stated that "thousands" of black people attended.

"In the forties I used to go on Sunday to see the blacks dance. They were given a large Square called Congo green where they indulged in dancing with music made by thumping on the head of a barrel with skin stretched over it. The performer would thump on it and carry on a chant. Another would beat the sides with two cobs or sticks. The dancers used to wear pieces of tin or some substitute on their legs to make a sort of jingle. I judged it was African music. The people looked as they, most of them, were the imported article."

–James Thomas, African descendant, traveler, 1840s

587. (*a*) Whereas, numerous citizens have requested the council of Municipality No. One, to grant permission to slaves to assemble on Sundays on Circus square, for the purpose of dansing.

Whereas, when such a merriment takes place before sunset and is not offensive to public decency, it can be tolerated: provided, it be under the police inspection.

Resolved that from the 1st of May to the 31st of August of each year, the slaves, provided with a written consent of their master, be permitted to assemble Sundays on the Circus square for the purpose of dancing from 4 till 6½ o'clock, P. M.

Resolved that it shall be the duty of the commissaries of police of the 3rd and 5th wards, of the commanding officer at Post Trémé and five men of the day police, to watch that no police ordinance be violated during the time allowed to negroes to dance on Circus square.

(*a*) Ord. 28 April 1845. Jour.

Ordinance that restored the Sunday gatherings in 1845

Several people who witnessed the events mentioned that the gatherers formed circles in different parts of the Square. Each circle had dancers, drummers, and other musicians inside. Drummers set the beat for each circle and other musicians joined in, plucking kalimbas, striking balaphons, picking banzas, and more. They played different rhythms at the same time, playing one against the other, making some beats long and others short, some loud and others softer, some strong and others weak. Musicians cleverly fit the music together, creating as they went along. They made the music travel through time and everybody in the circle with it.

Those who stood around to make up the circles participated too. They sang along with the leaders, responding to their calls. They clapped, patted, shook gourd rattles, and waited for their turn to dance. Reportedly, children danced on the outskirts of the circles, imitating the adults and adding their laughter and playfulness to the festive event.

SCENES IN CONGO SQUARE.—*Regular Ethiopian Break-Downs.*—Any one who says that the thousands of negroes congregated in and about Congo Square on Sunday afternoon last were unhappy we put down as no judge of human physiognomy. Some two or three weeks since an ordinance was passed restoring to them their ancient privilege of resorting thither, and thither they now repair in countless throngs. Rude instruments of their own contrivance, the like of which we have never seen before, were being played on Sunday last with a zeal that showed the enthusiasm of the performers, while sets of dancers were shuffling and breaking down upon the green sward with an earnestness that knew no tiring. Hour after hour, and

"Scenes in Congo Square," *Daily Picayune*, June 24, 1845

Sketch of couple dancing by E. W. Kemble

"Groups of fifties and hundreds may be seen in different sections of the square, with banjos, tom-toms, violins, jawbones, triangle, and various other instruments. . . ."

–James Creecy, traveler, 1834

"Blowing the Quills" by E. W. Kemble from the "Dance in Place Congo" article by George W. Cable

Perhaps best known for designing portions of the U.S. Capitol building, Benjamin Henry Latrobe was one of the first formally trained architects in the United States. He spent his last years in New Orleans designing the city's waterworks system.

Musical Instruments

African music, songs, and dances called for African-styled musical instruments. To make them, musicians used materials that they found in nature or items that were no longer in use, and they fashioned them like the ones they knew in their homelands. The main instrument was the drum, which musicians made in different sizes, shapes, and styles. Musicians made drums from hollowed logs and empty barrels, and every circle of dancers had one or more of them. Architect Benjamin Latrobe witnessed a gathering in 1819. He wrote about what he saw and drew pictures of some of the musical instruments. One of his illustrations depicts a drummer sitting astride his drum. When positioned in this manner, drummers play with their hands and frequently pressed the heel of one foot against the drum's head to alter the pitch. This style of drumming is associated with people from the Kongo-Angola region of Africa and was observed in other parts of Louisiana, as well as different parts of the African diaspora.

In addition to the other examples of instruments shown here, gatherers used their bodies as instruments. They patted their feet, slapped their thighs and chests, and clapped

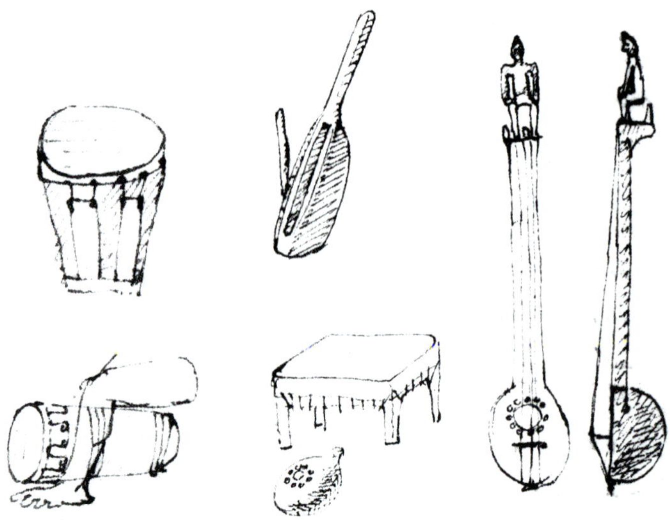

Sketches of instruments that Benjamin Latrobe saw in Congo Square

From left to right:

Drum made from empty barrel

Balaphon

Kalimba

Congolese-style drum, which a drummer straddled while playing

Flute made from bamboo

Slit drum, carved from log

Rattles made from gourds

Jawbone of a mule

Panpipes

Banza, string instrument made with a gourd; one of many variations of the instrument Latrobe observed in 1819

in beat to the music. Some gatherers struck cowbells and tapped and scraped dried jawbones of mules with sticks to make the loose teeth rattle. Male dancers sometimes attached pieces of metal to their clothing to produce jingling sounds when they danced.

Over time, particularly during the American period, gatherers added instruments with styles of European origin. These included the Jew's harp (also called jaw harp), triangle, tambourine, and violin (fiddle), also known as the cremona. Yet, African-styled instruments remained central to the music at Congo Square. Those instruments were evidence of the African influence on New Orleans-born music, including jazz and American-born performance styles, such as minstrelsy.

"A man sung a . . . song to the dancing which I suppose was in some African language, for it was not French."

–Benjamin Latrobe, architect, 1819

The Songs

People who gathered in Congo Square sang different songs over the years, including songs in African languages. However, Louisiana Creole, a language that combined terms from French and African languages, created a common language for residents of the colony, and it was the language of most of the known songs of Congo Square. Known as Creole slave songs or Creole folk songs, these included "Belle Layotte," "Musieu Bainjo," and "Aurore Pradère." Songs in English were also sung at the gatherings including "Old Virginia Never Tire," "Hey Jim Along," and "Get Along Home You Yallow Gals."

Regardless of the changes in language, certain African singing styles continued. One of them was "call and response," which involved a leader and one or more other singers. In this style, the leader sang a phrase and others followed by singing the same or different set phrase. The leader "called" and the followers "responded." Singers often made up songs or added words on the spot, which is called improvisation. The singers used their voices, their natural musical instruments, to dress-up or embellish simple melodies. They made their voices slide from one note to another and added notes to the melody called trills. This practice was called ornamentation. Later, jazz musicians made their instruments—trumpets, clarinets, trombones, and saxophones—do the same thing that singers did with their voices.

The following song includes words from an African language. It is one of the many songs that originated in Saint-Domingue (Haiti), where it was sung at Vodou ceremonies.

Eh! eh! Bomba!
Heu! heu!
Canga! fa o té!
Canga, monne dé lé!
Canga, do ki la!
Canga li!

Songs with melodies built on the habanera rhythm and its variations were popular at the gatherings. An example is the following Creole slave song, "Quan Patate La Cuite" (also "Quan Patate Latchuite"). During the American period, writers referred to this song more than any other. It is another song that came to New Orleans from Saint-Domingue (now Haiti), and it accompanied two popular dances—the Congo dance and the Bamboula dance.

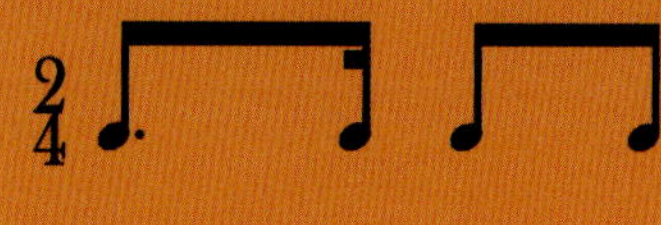

The habanera rhythm

Creole
"Quan Patate-Latchuite"
Quan patate-la tchuite.
Na nanan li, na nanan li.
Quan même li dans sirop.
Quan même li dans la soupe.
Quan même li dans chaudiere.
Quan même li dans la cendé
Na nanan li, na nannan li.
Na nanan li, na nannan li.

English
"When That Sweet Potato Will Be Cooked"
When that sweet potato will be cooked.
We will eat it, we will eat it.
Even if it is cooked in syrup.
Even if it is cooked in the soup.
Even if it is cooked in the pot.
Even if it is cooked in the ashes.
We will eat it, we will eat it.
We will eat it, we will eat it.

The following song, "Quand mo te jeune (Bal ni)," which means, "When I was Young (The End of the Ball)," was often sung at sunset when the gatherings ended. Mu-

Creole slave song "Quan Patate La Cuite," music notation written by Clara Peterson

The popular Cajun song "Allons danser Colinda," which is about a boy asking a girl named Colinda to dance close to him while her mother is away, derived from the Calinda dance and is an example of African cultural influence.

In the early 1720s, Le Page du Pratz observed three to four hundred enslaved Africans dance a Calinda on Sundays at the King's Plantation located in Algiers. There was also buying and selling.

sicians played drums and other instruments while other gatherers sang and performed a Calinda dance. The words tell that life, pleasure, and good times pass away quickly, so enjoy them when you can.

Creole
"Quand mo te jeune"
Quand mo-té jeun'
Mo-té jonglé Michieu;
A c't'heur ma-pé vini vieux
Mo-pé jonglé bon Dieu.

Ma-pé jonglé bon temps passé,
Ma-pé jonglé bon temps passé,
Ma-pé jonglé bon temps passé,
Ma-pé jonglé bon temps qu'est passé.

Le bal ni, bonsoir, Messieurs,
Le bal ni, bonsoir,
Mesdam' M'al-lé parti,
La, la, la, la, la

English
"When I was Young"
When I was young
Merry was I, dear Sirs.
And now when I am old
I still will merry be.

I will be gay for pleasure flies.
I will be gay for pleasure flies.
I will be gay for 'good times' pass away,
I will be gay for 'good times' pass away.

The dance is done, Goodnight Messieurs.
The dance is done, Goodnight Madames.
I go, I go!
La, la, la, la,

Sketch of a fiddler by E. W. Kemble

A painting of a Calinda dance in the Americas by François Aimé Louis Dumoulin, c. 1783

"The dancers are most fancifully dressed with fringes, ribbons, little bells, and shells, and balls, jingling and flirting about the performer's legs and arms, who sing a second or counter to the music most sweetly. . . . Young and old join in the sport and dances.

"When a dancer or danseuse surpasses expectation, or is particularly brilliant in the execution of 'flings' and 'flourishings' of limb and body, shouts huzzas, and clapping of hands follow, and numerous picallions are thrown in the ring to the performers by (strange) spectators."

James Creecy, traveler, 1834

The Dances

Several dances performed in Congo Square were the same or similar to those performed in parts of West and Central West Africa and the French and Spanish West Indies—particularly Haiti and Cuba. One of those was the Calinda, which Africans performed in New Orleans beginning in the early 1720s. Several versions of the Calinda existed. One version was performed in a circle and the other in two lines that faced each other. Another version was a war-like, mock stick-fighting dance.

The dance that most writers told about during the American period was the Congo dance, which came from the Kongo/Angola people. During the dance, women often held handkerchiefs or the corners of aprons by their fin-

Johann Buechler, who traveled to New Orleans in the spring of 1817, witnessed enslaved blacks dancing behind the city on Sunday starting around four o'clock at different, large open spaces. He later traveled to Cuba, where he witnessed the same kind of dancing every Sunday after supper.

Capoeira or "Dance of War," by Johann Moritz Rugendas depicts a war dance in Cuba, 1835

"Bamboula," a bomba-style performance featuring Militeri Tucker Concepcion, dancer and William "Billy T" Tucker, drummer, 2015

The Bamboula by E. W. Kemble, 1880

gertips. A drummer often straddled or sat across his drum while playing with his hands, fingers, and the heel of one foot. This drumming style and dance, or versions of it, were also popular in other places where enslaved people from the West central region of Africa had been taken, including Haiti, Cuba, Puerto Rico, Jamaica, and Brazil.

The Bamboula dance was closely related to the Congo dance and the names may have been used interchangeably. There were similar movements for males and females, and the same song and musical instruments accompanied them. In such cases, the dances are said to be cousins. The Creole slave song that accompanied both was "Quan Patate La Cuite" (also "Quan Patate Latchuite").

Edward Kemble's depiction of the Bamboula dance has become an iconic representation of the dance as well as the most popular representation of the gatherings in Congo Square. However, Kemble never witnessed the gatherings. He created his sketchs for an article that George Washing-

"Those who know the weird liet-motif of Coleridge-Taylor's Bamboula dance have heard the tune of the Congo dance, which every child in New Orleans could sing."

–Alice Dunbar-Nelson, African American, Poet, Journalist, 1916

Playbill for Pell's Serenaders, featuring "Boz's Juba" at a Birmingham theater in 1848

William Henry Lane (1825-1852) received the name "Master Juba" because of his skillful dancing, which influenced a new style called tap dance. Also known as "Boz's Juba," Lane used his body as a musical instrument and blended African rhythms and dance movements with European jigs, reels, and clog dance styles. He was among the first black performers to tour with white minstrel performers—all of whom painted their faces with burnt cork, called blackface.

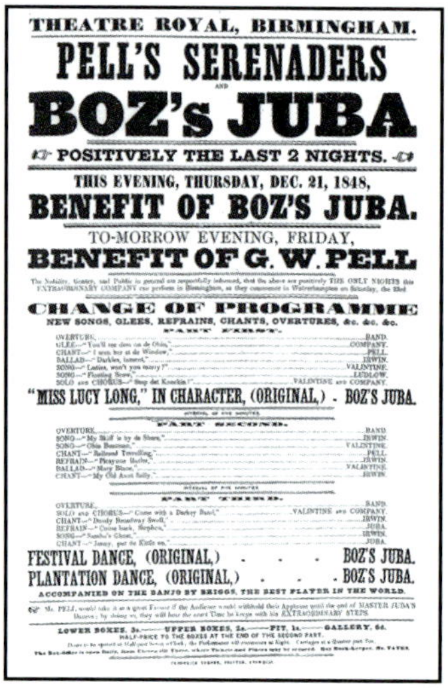

THEATRE ROYAL, BIRMINGHAM.

PELL'S SERENADERS

AND

BOZ's JUBA

POSITIVELY THE LAST 2 NIGHTS.

THIS EVENING, THURSDAY, DEC. 21, 1848,

BENEFIT OF BOZ'S JUBA.

TO-MORROW EVENING, FRIDAY,

BENEFIT OF G. W. PELL

CHANGE OF PROGRAMME

NEW SONGS, GLEES, REFRAINS, CHANTS, OVERTURES, &c. &c. &c.

PART FIRST.

"MISS LUCY LONG," IN CHARACTER, (ORIGINAL,) - BOZ'S JUBA.

PART SECOND.

PART THIRD.

FESTIVAL DANCE, (ORIGINAL,) . . . . BOZ'S JUBA.

PLANTATION DANCE, (ORIGINAL,) . . . . BOZ'S JUBA.

ACCOMPANIED ON THE BANJO BY BRIGGS, THE BEST PLAYER IN THE WORLD.

LOWER BOXES, 3s.——UPPER BOXES, 2s.——PIT, 1s.——GALLERY, 6d.

HALF-PRICE TO THE BOXES AT THE END OF THE SECOND PART.

Right: A sketch of William Henry Lane "Master Juba" performing in blackface

ton Cable published in *Century Magazine* in 1880, decades after the gatherings ended. In his depiction, he opened up the dance circle to allow the audience to look inside.

The Juba dance also began with people from the Kongo nation, many of whom speak the Ki Kongo language. The word "juba" comes from the Ki Kongo word "zuba," which means "to slap." The dance itself came from a thigh-slapping dance in the Kongo called nzuba. Black people not only danced Juba in Congo Square but throughout Louisiana and across the country—particularly the South. Several new dance styles evolved from it. In some places, a variation of the Juba became known as Hambone, which was a dance as well as a thigh and chest patting game and is still performed today. Tap dancing also grew out of the Juba dance, and minstrel performers like E. P. Christy performed their version of the Juba dance in New York on Broadway and on other stages around the country.

Other dances performed in Congo Square included the Chacta (Cata), Counjaille, and the Carabine. As enslaved African Americans entered New Orleans during the domestic slave trade, they increasingly introduced European dance styles that called for English-based songs. Yet, according to newspaper articles and eyewitnesses, the performance of African-based dances and musical instruments continued. New Orleanians and travelers to the city observed carryovers and evidence of those African dances and musical instruments into the mid 1900s.

"Leaving the basin [the Carondelet Canal], we passed a treeless green, which we were informed by a passer-by, was dignified by the classical appellation of 'Congo Square.' Here our obliging informant gave us to understand, the coloured 'ladies and gentlemen' are accustomed to assemble on gala and saints days, and to the time of outlandish music, dance, not the Romaika, alas! But the 'Fandango!'"

–Joseph Holt Ingraham, traveler, 1835

Danny "Slapjazz" Barber, a master of traditional Hambone body percussion, and Sekani Thomas slapping Hambone. Photo by Sherwood Chen

On Sunday afternoon, "in the rear of the town . . . the sight of twenty different dancing groups of . . . Africans, collected together to perform their worship after the manner of their country."

–Christian Schultz, traveler, 1808

"Wherever the African is, there is his religion for, he carries it to the fields, the beer party, a funeral ceremony, and even the house of parliament if he is a politician."

–John Mbiti, African philosopher, historian, 1969

Spirituality and Religion

Enslaved Africans brought their religions with them from their homelands to Louisiana. However, Article II of the Code Noir mandated slaveholders to baptize them, which means to also instruct them, in the Catholic faith. Some of the Africans, particularly those from the Kongo may have already been exposed, if not converted, to the Catholic faith as missionaries taught and baptized people in that country beginning in the fifteenth century. In Louisiana, although many of the Africans did become Catholic, their traditional beliefs remained a part of who they were. Many of them in Louisiana and other locations like Saint-Domingue (Haiti), where the same laws existed, practiced parts of more than one religion. Some practiced Catholicism in public and parts of their traditional religions in private and at gathering places like Congo Square.

Traveler Christian Schultz witnessed an African practice at a Sunday gathering in 1808. He noticed that a number of tails from small wild animals hung from the clothing of some of the lead dancers. The leaders who looked the most horrible or most decorated always had the largest number of people in their circles.

In what is now the Democratic Republic of the Congo, in West Central Africa, people who dressed in that manner are called ritual specialists or diviners. The animal tails that they wore hanging from their waist stood for nkisi, which are. Ritual specialists use those spirits and medicines to heal people and bring good luck to them. In Congo Square, the gatherers who followed those leaders believed that when the leaders danced and spun around, the animal tails flew out and spread protection over them and over the diviner.

Those gatherers were seeking more than just a good time. They were practicing their beliefs and seeking help from a source greater than themselves. Those practices and

Diviner from Katanga, Congo, wearing animal tails hanging from his waistline, 2006. Photo by Jacques Janqoux

beliefs were not just seen in Congo Square or New Orleans or Louisiana. People throughout the South held similar beliefs. Ritual specialists became known as roots people or conjurors. Nkisi became known as magical charms, wanga, or gris-gris. Some people wore such objects on parts of their body or kept them in secret places. People from the Kongo/Angola region of Africa are credited with giving the system of medicines to the Vodou religion, which many people in New Orleans practiced.

Vodou (also Voudou, Voodoo) is a religion that developed among enslaved people who combined practices from the Catholic faith with practices and beliefs from African religions—particularly those held by the Yoruba, Kongo, and Fon people. The name "Vodou" came from "Vodun," a word from the Fon people that means "spirit" or "Gods." Vodou is an established religion, however many variations and definitions of it exist today.

Marie Laveau, often referred to as the "Vodou Queen of New Orleans," was a prominent free woman of color and renowned practitioner of Vodou.

In the market, "Negro women in bright bandanas, and otherwise neatly dressed, presided over tables, and were evidently the popular traders; and these were slaves, laughing and chatting, and apparently as free as a customer who ordered his omelet or fruit; and I learned consequently that these women represented their owners."

–Ellen Call Long, traveler

Buying and Selling

Wherever the Sunday gatherings took place, there was buying and selling. Enslaved people bought and sold what they grew in their garden patches, like rice, hunted in the swamps, like rabbits, caught fishing, gathered from nature, such as wild berries, and made in their kitchens such as pies and pralines. A newspaper article stated that the market thrived. In part, credit for its success goes to the free people of color and white spectators who came with money, but enslaved people came with money too. The Sunday events provided an opportunity for them to spend what they had earned and sell items that they had acquired during their time off. At the core of the market were buyers as well as sellers who were enslaved.

Although there were male marketers, it was no surprise that market women were very popular. The women brought the tradition of marketing and their spirit for business with them from Africa. Not only were they popular at Congo Square, market women dominated small-scale sales called "petty marketing" throughout the city. Most of them spoke several languages and handled business in whichever one their customers demanded, including African dialects, French, Creole, Spanish, and English.

In the city, market women set up stands in pubic markets, on street corners, and the levee, walked up and down sidewalks and alleys, and knocked on doors of houses and busi-

Woman selling pralines

nesses. Many of them worked for their owners to whom they gave the money that they made. Also among them were free women of color, some of whom had earned and stored away enough money to purchase their freedom. This was true of Rose Nichaud, who is reported to have been the first coffee vendor in the city. She operated her stand in Jackson Square outside the St. Louis Cathedral.

In Congo Square, some market women spread their goods on the ground. Others used tables and stands, and some of them walked in and out of crowds with their goods in baskets balanced on their heads. As they walked, they chanted about the items they had for sale. One popular food item was calas (kah-lah), deep-fried rice cakes sprinkled with powdered sugar. Women who sold these at breakfast time and throughout the day often sang the following street cry or chant to advertise their calas as they walked along. *Belle* means beautiful, and *tout chaud* means all hot.

Belle Ca..las…!
Tout chaud.
All hot.
Get 'em while they're hot.

Belle Ca..las…!
Tout chaud.
All hot.
Get'em while they're hot.

Sketch of woman selling calas

Popular items also included roasted peanuts, popcorn, pecan pies, pralines made with pecans, and peanuts. There were cakes, molasses candy, coconut candy, and gingerbread treats known as stage planks. Beverages included lemonade, hot coffee, and Louisiana rum called tafia. The most popular beverage was *la bierre du pays*. It was also known as spruce beer, ginger beer, and Creole beer, and it was non-alcoholic.

Enslaved men and women sold items that they found in nature like driftwood from along the Mississippi River, moss from trees to pad furniture and mattresses, bundles of sticks for firewood, and buckets of ashes to make soap. The following song lyrics identify more items. The composer of this Creole folk song may have lived in the "back-of-town" area of the city near Congo Square. The lyrics mention that they visited a location on St. Ann Street, which borders the Square.

Fried rice fritters called calas "originated in Liberia. Like its counterpart the acarajé, it has an African-sounding name, because kala means rice in the Vai language of Liberia, and its neighbor, Sierra Leone."

–Jessica Harris, from "Foodways to Freedom," *American Legacy Woman*, 2003

Creole

Pitis sans popa, pitis sans moman,
Qui ça 'ou' zut' fé pou' gagnein l'a'zanc,
No courri l'aut' bord pou' cercé patt c'at'
No tournein bayou pou' péc'é patassa;
Et v'là comm ça no té fé nou' l'a'zanc.

Pitis sans popa, pitis sans moman,
Qui ça 'ou' zut' fé pou' gagnein l'a'zanc,
No courri dans bois fouillé latanié

No vend' so racin' pou' fou'bi' planç'é;
Et v'là comm' ça no té fé nou' l'a'zanc.

Pitis sans popa, pitis sans moman,
Qui ça 'ou' zut' fé pou' gagnein l'a'zanc,
Pou' fé di thé n'a fouillé sassaf'as,
Pou' fé di l'enc' no po'té grain' sougras;
Et v'là comm ça no té fé nou' l'a'zanc.

Pitis sans popa, pitis sans moman,
Qui ça 'ou' zut' fé pou' gagnein l'a'zanc,
No courri dans bois ramassé cancos;
Avé nou' la caze no trappé zozos;

Et v'là comm ça no té fé nou' l'a'zanc,

Pitis sans popa, pitis sans moman,
Qui ça 'ou' zut' fé pou' gagnein l'a'zanc,
No courri à soir c'ez Mom'selle Maroto,
Dans la rie St. Ann ou no té zoué loto;
Et v'là comm ça no té fé nou' l'a'za

English*
Little ones without father, little ones without mother,
What do you do to earn money?
The river we cross for wild berries to search;
We follow the bayou a'fishing for perch;
And that's how we earn money.

Little ones without father, little ones without mother,
What do you do to earn money?
Palmetto we dig from the swamp's bristling stores
And sell its stout root for scrubbing the floors;
And that's how we earn money.

Little ones without father, little ones without mother,
What do you do to earn money?
The sassafras root we dig up; it makes tea;
For ink the ripe pokeberry clusters bring we;
And that's how we earn money

Little ones without father, little ones without mother,
What do you do to earn money?
We go to the woods cancos berries to fetch,
And in our trap cages the birds we catch;
And that's how we earn money.

Little ones without father, little ones without mother,
What do you do to earn money?
At evening we visit Mom'selle Maroto,
In St. Ann's Street, to gamble awhile at keno;
And that's how we earn money.

*Translated by Gwendolyn Midlo Hall

"In visiting the provision markets of New Orleans, an intelligent traveler must be surprised at seeing almost the whole of purchasing and selling the edible articles for domestic consumption, transacted by colored persons. Our butchers are negroes, our fishmongers negroes, our venders of vegetables, fruit and flowers are all negroes—but what is worse with very few exceptions the only purchasers that frequent the markets are negroes; and generally slaves. It is true that a few white women who keep boarding houses are occasionally seen; but it is too true that the responsible duty of purchasing every species of market provision for the use of families is confided to the slaves, who are at liberty to purchase what they please, how they please, and where they please without the personal inspection of any member of the family."

–*The Bee*, October 13, 1835

5

The Influence of the Gatherings

The people who gathered in Congo Square and at other locations in the city hundreds of years ago laid the foundation for some of the cultural practices that are indigenous to New Orleans, including jazz music, second lines, and the music of Mardi Gras Indians. The ability to trace practices that are happening today back to those that happened hundreds of years ago allows people to connect the present to the past and understand how historical events impact our lives.

New Orleans's carnival season developed from Catholic processional traditions in the European and enslaved communities. The Rex organization was founded and began parading in 1872. It, along with the Krewe of Zulu (founded by black New Orleans residents in the early twentieth century), remain the principle parades on Mardi Gras day in New Orleans.

When looking at the influence of New Orleans's music, it is important to note that many black musicians, enslaved and free, played and encountered numerous styles of music—including African-styles. Some composed and played classical or European-style music. One of them was Basile Jean Bares, a pianist and composer who was enslaved and perhaps the most popular entertainer in New Orleans in the 1860s and 1870s. He and his band played for Rex, the king of carnival, and for other carnival balls. Bares wrote and performed marches, waltzes, polkas, gallops, quadrilles, and mazurkas. Some of his compositions included the habanera rhythm and variations of it, as seen in his piece "Los Campanillas."

Edmond, another enslaved musician, played clarinet at balls and parties held for free people of color, where basically the same kind of music was performed. When Edmond ran away from his owner in 1847, the runaway ad stated that he played drums for a military company as well. As with Jordan Noble, "Old Jordan," who also drummed for military drills during that time, scholars presume that they were with white militia units. Bares and Edmond were among many other musicians who were enslaved and who performed in bands and ensembles with musicians who were free.

"Los Campanillas" composed and hand-written by Basile Bares, when he was enslaved

Harrison, who played violin, was also enslaved. He may have played music that would have been in Congo Square, or classical music in bands with free people of color, or both. In other words, New Orleans was a melting pot of musical styles, and black musicians, enslaved and free, played and shared a wide variety of them, including the African rhythms, military marches, Creole slave songs, the blues, spasm bands, church music, jigs, rags (ragtime), opera, and the styles mentioned above (i.e. waltzes, polkas, gallops, quadrilles, and mazurkas).

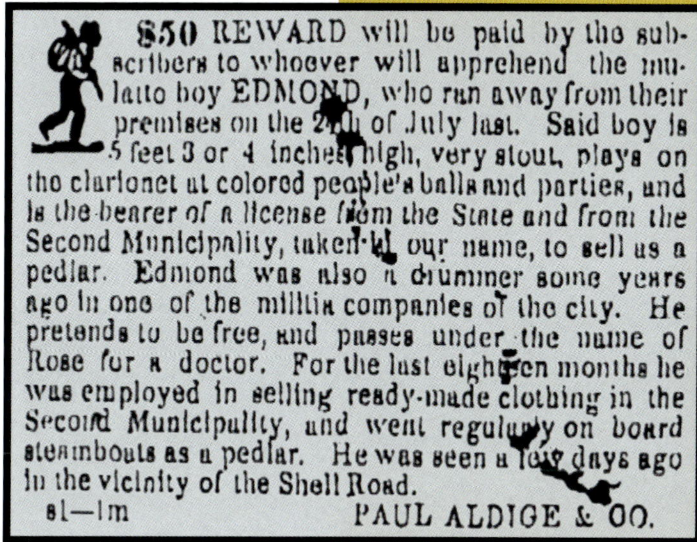

$50 REWARD will be paid by the subscribers to whoever will apprehend the mulatto boy EDMOND, who ran away from their premises on the 2[illegible]th of July last. Said boy is 5 feet 3 or 4 inches high, very stout, plays on the clarionet at colored people's balls and parties, and is the bearer of a license from the State and from the Second Municipality, taken in our name, to sell as a pedlar. Edmond was also a drummer some years ago in one of the militia companies of the city. He pretends to be free, and passes under the name of Rose for a doctor. For the last eighteen months he was employed in selling ready-made clothing in the Second Municipality, and went regularly on board steamboats as a pedlar. He was seen a few days ago in the vicinity of the Shell Road.

s1—1m PAUL ALDIGE & CO.

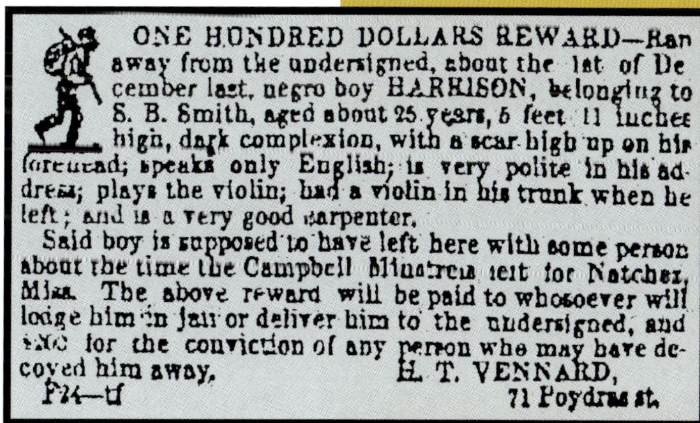

ONE HUNDRED DOLLARS REWARD—Ran away from the undersigned, about the 1st of December last, negro boy HARRISON, belonging to S. B. Smith, aged about 25 years, 5 feet 11 inches high, dark complexion, with a scar high up on his forehead; speaks only English; is very polite in his address; plays the violin; had a violin in his trunk when he left; and is a very good carpenter.

Said boy is supposed to have left here with some person about the time the Campbell Minstrels left for Natchez, Miss. The above reward will be paid to whosoever will lodge him in jail or deliver him to the undersigned, and $200 for the conviction of any person who may have decoyed him away.

H. T. VENNARD,
F24—tf 71 Poydras st.

Top: Runawayad for Edmond, *Daily Picayune*, September 11, 1847

Bottom: Runaway ad for Harrison, *Daily Picayune*, May 8, 1854

Musicians who moved to the city joined in with the styles that existed and introduced new ones. In addition to the different regions in Africa, some of them had arrived from parts of the Caribbean such as Haiti and Cuba and places within the United States, including Virginia and Maryland. After emancipation, black people, including musicians from rural areas and surrounding states, fled to New Orleans. Those musicians brought their styles of playing, most of which carried the same African practices, such as polyrhythms (playing several rhythms at the same time), improvisation, call and response, ornamentation, and more. Over time, the blending of experiences and styles of black musicians in the city resulted in new styles—New Orleans styles. That blending planted the seeds for what became New Orleans jazz in the late 1890s and the beginning of the 1900s.

Jazz Music

Many early jazz musicians acquired instruments second-hand, particularly military instruments such as the cornet, a shorter and more conical version of the trumpet.

The elements, or key characteristics, of the music that came to be called jazz were present in the music that gatherers created on Sundays in Congo Square. However, black musicians included those elements in their music at other locations in New Orleans and other parts of the country. Although Congo Square was not the only place for such African-based music, it was important. It was a public location where hundreds, sometimes into a thousand, black gatherers from different settings and a wide range of backgrounds and musical experiences freely congregated. They performed African-derived dances and African rhythms on African-based instruments over a long span of time and at relatively late dates in time. The many reports that document the gatherings add to the location's significance. Dena J. Epstein concluded after her research on African music in the Americas that, "Only in Place Congo in New Orleans was the African tradition able to continue in the open."

A cartoon appearing in the New Orleans newspaper *The Mascot* in 1890, demonstrated that not all New Orleanians were open to the changing musical landscape of their city.

Those gatherings impacted generations of musicians and dancers who passed down practices and kept them alive. Available documents suggest that the public gatherings for enslaved people ended in the 1850s, but opportunities for free people of color may have existed longer. When the public gatherings for enslaved people ended in Congo Square, meetings of any sort and for any purpose were banned to the point of beatings and jail time. In spite of the risks, when and wherever possible, meetings sometimes took place in small numbers in private locations, including houses, taverns, and backyards. After emancipation, public dances resumed in Congo Square and elsewhere. New Orleans-born musician, composer, and writer of African heritage, Camille Nickerson, affirmed that the dances continued in New Orleans long after the gatherings in Place Congo ended. These events, sometimes called Creole dances, included popular singing and musical instruments as well as familiar food items, such as calas, slices of pains patatte (sweet potato pudding), pralines, and pineapple beer. The cultural practices at the Sunday gatherings in Congo Square clearly influenced New Orleans popular culture.

Oscar "Papa" Celestin performed with his band at the first New Orleans Jazz Festival, sponsored by the New Orleans Jazz Club, held at Congo Square in 1949.

Like seeds planted in rich soil, the African and African-based music and dance prevalent in Congo Square and other locations penetrated the fiber of New Orleans. They engaged with an array of musical cultures that originated around the world and over time blossomed into new music and dance styles, including traditional New Orleans jazz. Music historians pinpoint the last decade of the nineteenth century and the first decade of the twentieth century as the years that jazz developed.

One of the key elements of jazz that musicians passed down was the habanera rhythm. It was sometimes referred to as the tango bass line and the Spanish Tinge—although it originated in Africa. Ferdinand Morton, known as Jelly Roll Morton, born in 1890, was one

Some of New Orleans's most notable early jazz musicians include:

- Buddy Bolden (1877-1931), cornet
- Freddie Keppard (1889-1933), cornet
- Joseph Nathan "King" Oliver (1881-1938), trumpet and composer
- Louis "Satchmo" Armstrong (1901-1971), cornet, trumpet, and vocalist
- Oscar "Papa" Celestin (1884-1954), trumpet and vocalist
- Edward "Kid" Ory (1886-1973), trombone and bandleader
- "Jelly Roll" Morton (1890-1941), piano and composer
- Sidney Bechet (1897-1959), clarinet
- George Lewis (1900-1968), clarinet and composer

Ferdinand "Jelly Roll" Morton

Jazz continues to play a major role in New Orleans's culture. Today, prominent musicians include:

Above: Dr. Michael White (1954-) a clarinetist, educator, composer, and descendant of first generation jazz musicians. He works to preserve, perpetuate, and expand the traditional New Orleans jazz style through international performances, recordings, publications, and public programs for general audiences.

Right: Wynton Marsalis (1961-), a trumpet player, composer, teacher, music educator, and artistic director of Jazz at Lincoln Center in New York City. He debuted his composition "Congo Square" in Congo Square in 2006.

of the earliest jazz musicians in New Orleans. He stated that this rhythm had to be present if the music was to be called jazz. When Morton published his piano composition, "Jelly Roll Blues," he became the first person to write and publish jazz music.

Sheetmusic for Jelly Roll Morton's "Jelly Roll Blues"

The habanera rhythm and variations of it were also popular in ragtime music and the blues, which were styles that also began with black musicians. One of the variations of the habanera is the three-note pattern called the tresillo in Cuba. In New Orleans, it is called the second line beat. It is the foundational rhythm of so much New Orleans music that

Second line beat

it is also called the street beat, the bamboula beat, the parade beat, and the New Orleans beat. It is the heart of the music for jazz funerals, the music that brass bands play at second line parades for benevolent societies and social aid and pleasure clubs, and the music of Mardi Gras Indians.

When writing and speaking about the beginnings of jazz, historians mention Congo Square more often than any other location. New Orleans-born musicians like Louis Armstrong, who was born in 1901 and began playing the cornet at age thirteen, helped to make jazz popular around the country and the world. Now performed on every continent, jazz is considered to be America's gift to the world.

Because of the role that Congo Square played in the development of the music, UNESCO (United Nations Educational, Scientific and Cultural Organizations) launched the first International Jazz Day at the historic site in 2012, with jazz performances taking place that day in over 190 countries.

Louis Armstrong at the New Orleans International Jazz Fest in1968

The first New Orleans Jazz and Heritage Festival was held in 1970 in Congo Square. It featured New Orleans native Mahalia Jackson, who acknowledged the influence of New Orleans music on her style as a gospel singer.

Singer Michaela Harrison, drummer Luther Gray, dancer Jamilah Peters-Muhammad, and members of the Congo Square Preservation Society in Congo Square, 1st International Jazz Day, April 30, 2012

Members of Black Men of Labor Social Aid and Pleasure Club lead a jazz funeral for Attorney Lolis Elie, April 8, 2017

Jazz Funerals

Jazz funerals, a cultural practice that is indigenous to New Orleans, received influence from West African burial traditions and music along with European-styled military bands. First referred to as "funerals with music," they are used to honor deceased musicians, members of clubs, and distinguished members of the community. During processions or marches from the church to the gravesite, bands play a dirge, a slow and sad funeral song, such as "Just a Closer Walk with Thee." On the return, bands play rousing and upbeat songs such as "Didn't He Ramble" and "When the Saints Go Marching In."

Benevolent associations, organizations within the community that provide assistance to members, and Social Aid and Pleasure Clubs, also based on membership, often provide funerals with music for their deceased members. These organizations help their members during illness and death, perform community service or charitable work, and sponsor social events such as picnics, dinners, balls, and an annual parade.

Andre Cailloux (1825-1863) was born enslaved in New Orleans and obtained his freedom in 1846. Cailloux fought for the Union Army during the Civil War and was one of the first black Union Army officers to be killed in combat, which quickly made him a hero among black people in Louisiana. His body was returned to New Orleans where one of the largest funeral processions for a person of color accompanied his body through Congo Square. He was interred in St. Louis Cemetery #2.

Brass band playing at a jazz funeral in the Tremé neighborhood that ended in Congo Square

The brass band tradition in New Orleans draws from European and African performance styles and is basic to the city's musical culture. Brass bands provide the music for jazz funerals, second line parades, weddings, parties, and so on. They typically include a tuba, trombone, trumpet, clarinet and/or saxophone, snare drum, and bass drum.

Second Line Parades

The annual parades of benevolent associations and social aid and pleasure clubs are known as second line parades. The second line tradition of parading in the streets is indigenous to New Orleans and dates back to the late 1800s.

Parades include the "main line" or "first line," which are the members of the parading club along with a brass band. People who follow the band to support the club and to enjoy the experience are called the "second line." Second lines usually grow in size as parades wind their way through neighborhoods and attract more people.

Today, dressed in color-coordinated finery from head to toe, club members strut, high-step,

Sons of Hope and the Annual Parade of the Young Veterans, painting by John Patrick Pemberton. Social Aid and Pleasure Club Parade, New Orleans, c. 1902

Members of Lady Buck Jumpers Social Aid and Pleasure Club, 30th Anniversary Parade, November 20, 2014

and buckjump through back streets of the city as scores of photographers from far and near swarm around them. Club members usually carry creatively designed and decorated fans and/or umbrellas embellished with bows, sequins, and fancy trim called marabou. Although there is a long tradition of male second line clubs, several female clubs also exist, including the Lady Buck Jumpers.

Some parades have themes and some pay tribute to specific people or causes. In 2011, the Black Men of Labor Social Aid and Pleasure Club paid tribute to the fiftieth anniversary of the Freedom Riders and dedicated the parade to the members of the New Orleans chapter of CORE (Congress for Racial Equality). The honorees included Don Hubbard, "Dodie" Smith Simmons, Jerome Smith, and Matt "Flukie" Suarez.

Some organizations, including the Young Men Olympian Junior Benevolent Association (YMO) create youth groups that engage children in the parading traditions. Founded in 1884, it is the oldest and only benevolent as-

During the "second line season," which begins the last week of August and continues until the middle of June, with breaks for holidays and the hottest part of summer, there are second line parades nearly every Sunday. Scheduled stops along the journey of several miles enable club members to refresh themselves with food and beverages.

sociation that holds yearly parades. In 2017, YMO celebrated 133 years of parading. That same year, more than forty-five social aid and pleasure clubs also brought African-based music and dance to neighborhood streets, festivals, and public and private events in New Orleans. Annual parades, jazz funerals, and gigs (i.e. tourism and other commercial enterprises, public and private entertainment, celebrations, and receptions) all serve to keep the second line parading tradition alive, vibrant, and diverse. The role of second line parades in continuing African-based expressions establishes another link to historic Congo Square, which previously served the same role. Like Congo Square, the second line parading tradition provides an opportunity for black New Orleanians to express a range of ideas and concepts that promote cultural identity, celebrate community, establish a sense of belonging, display ingenuity, and embrace the freedom to "do what cha wanna."

More than forty-five social aid and pleasure clubs, along with the Young Men Olympian Junior Benevolent Association parade each year. The New Orleans Jazz and Heritage Festival features second line clubs at the Fair Grounds each day of the festival to give visitors a taste of this New Orleans tradition.

Members of Young Men Olympian Junior Benevolent Association (YMO) lead jazz funeral for a deceased member, Alfred "Bucket" Carter. March 21, 2015, Lafayette Cemetery

The historic Tremé Neighborhood, founded in 1812, was a racially mixed neighborhood from its beginning and remains an important center of the city's African American culture. Many social aid and pleasure clubs wind their annual parades through the streets of Tremé where landmarks, including Congo Square, St. Augustine Catholic Church, and the Backstreet Cultural Museum, are located.

Second Line Dancing

The dancing was the main attraction for spectators at the Sunday gatherings. Grace King, who lived in New Orleans, wrote that the white people promenaded by to see the scene, and young men from the College of Orleans, en route to the theater, always stopped by to see the gatherers dance "Congo." Benjamin Latrobe witnessed two women dancing in one of the circles, each holding a handkerchief by her fingertips. Other writers also observed women in the city waving handkerchiefs or the corners of their aprons when dancing. Historian Robert Farris Thompson found that people of Kongo heritage waved handkerchiefs while dancing as an act of cleansing the air of evil spirits. They were symbolically sending problems away. People in other African countries also waved handkerchiefs when dancing as noted in photographs from Ghana and Nigeria.

Ibo women of southern Nigeria performing a traditional dance with white handkerchiefs

Girls dancing at an official public ceremony in Ho Ghana, Africa, 2006

Today, it is a New Orleans tradition among people of all races to wave handkerchiefs while second line dancing at parties, weddings, festivals, and at other events. Some also wave them at second line parades, which benevolent associations and social aid and pleasure clubs sponsor each year. Although members of those clubs often carry decorated fans or umbrellas that accent their outfits, it is not uncommon for their family and friends to receive and wave souvenir handkerchiefs. The name of the parading club and the date of the parade are often printed on the handkerchiefs to match the color scheme of the parade.

Second line dancers in New Orleans waving handkerchiefs

Known as the "chief of chiefs," Big Chief Allison "Tootie" Montana of the Yellow Pocahontas Black Masking Indian Tribe worked on suits and masked during Carnival until he was 82 years old, totaling 52 years of masking. He is regarded among Mardi Gras Indians as the chief who curtailed the violence in the Indian culture from that of fighting with fists to fighting with a needle and thread to make the prettiest suit. A sculpture in his honor stands in Louis Armstrong Park near Congo Square.

Music of the Mardi Gras Indians

The Mardi Gras Indian masking tradition is also indigenous to New Orleans. Mardi Gras Indians are black New Orleanians who form tribes/gangs/nations and mask or dress like Indians on Mardi Gras Day. Many people in the tradition say that masking as "Indians" started as a way to pay tribute or homage to Native Americans for assisting black people in various ways during slavery. On Mardi Gras Day, the last day of Carnival, Indians reveal the works of art, called suits, that they have worked on all year. Every year, those who mask invest hundreds to thousands of hours and dollars into a new suit.

Big Chief David Perry and Big Queen Keyshawna Jones, Wild Red Flame Mardi Gras Indians, Super Sunday, March 19, 2017

"Let's Go Git 'Em,"
Mardi Gras Indian call and response chant

Leader: The Call	The Response
Early in the morning	Let's go git 'em
Meet everybody	Let's go git 'em
Do what you wanna	Let's go git 'em
Have your fun now	Let's go git 'em
The leader creates.....	Let's go git 'em
" " "	

In 1999 Cherice Harrison-Nelson and Dr. Rosalyn Johnson Smith co-founded the Mardi Gras Indian Hall of Fame. Organized in honor of Big Chief Donald Harrison of the Guardians of the Flame Maroon Society, the Mardi Gras Indian Hall of Fame is a series of annual events designed to educate the general public about Mardi Gras Indians as well as perpetuate and celebrate the tradition.

The music, songs, and chants of Mardi Gras Indians show the impact of the Congo Square gatherings on the indigenous culture of today. The call and response singing or chanting, creating music on the spot (called improvisation), playing off beats or syncopation, playing of the tambourine, and using the three-beat rhythmic pattern known as the second line beat were all common practices at the gatherings in Congo Square. These practices are heard in classic Mardi Gras Indian recordings such as "Hey Pocky Way" by the Meters and on the streets when the tribes come out in their colorful and brilliantly designed suits on Mardi Gras Day. A chant that is sure to be heard among tribes is "We Won't Bow Down." It represents the spirit of the masking tradition and embodies the iconic second line rhythmic pattern.

Spy Boy Kerry and Queen Lorenza Lawless, Black Mohawk Mardi Gras Indians, Super Sunday, March 19, 2017

Marketing Traditions

Marketing existed at the Sunday afternoon gatherings long before Congo Square became the official gathering place. When Le Page du Pratz observed Sunday gatherings on the King's Plantation in the early 1720s, he noted that there was buying and selling. This economic exchange continued at other locations and was a central part of the gatherings in Congo Square. When those gatherings ended, the buying and selling continued wherever the gatherings did. For social aid and pleasure clubs, gatherings continued in the streets during their annual second line parades. There, the market people are known as vendors and the gatherers are known as second liners. Like the market women and men at Congo Square, the vendors provide a service to the clubs and second liners while making money for themselves.

Today, some vendors set up stands along parade routes, and some have movable equipment like ice chests on wheels that allow them to keep up with the parade. Pick-up trucks that pull barbeque pits and food trucks with a variety of items are now a part of the parade scene. Homemade goods like pralines, pies, and roasted peanuts, once sold in Congo Square, still prevail, but new products, such as Jell-O pops, add to the traditional offerings. The wide range of vendors receive ongoing support from the hundreds of second liners, who come from all races and backgrounds. New products and the new vending approaches all work together to keep the marketing tradition alive.

Loretta S. Harrison is the first black person in New Orleans history to advance from the level of "petty marketing" to owning and operating a candy manufacturing company. Ever innovative yet traditional, "Loretta's Authentic Pralines" offers a wide variety of delicacies that provide a taste of New Orleans.

National Impact

The influence of the gatherings at Congo Square also reached the national level. E. P. Christy, one of the most well known black-faced minstrel performers, lived in New Orleans during his young adult life and visited the Sunday gatherings every chance he got. He stated that the music and dance at "Congo Green," one of the names used for Congo Square, provided the material for his shows.

Christy and other minstrels painted their faces black and performed music and dances of enslaved people in degrading ways that mocked them and their culture. Christy developed a three-part show format that minstrel shows used around the country. He performed ten years in New York on Broadway, which brought him fame and lots of money. His troupe toured Europe and also performed in New Orleans. One of his acts was "The Congo Green dance," which he named after Congo Square. He also performed a version of the Juba dance, using the same name.

Some of the Creole slave songs also reached audiences around the county. In 1884-85, George Washington Cable and Mark Twain (Samuel L. Clemens) toured the United States and Canada together promoting their work, which was collecting and singing those songs. They called the songs "Creole African." One of the songs that Cable sang was "Quan Patate La Cuite," the popular song that accompanied the Congo dance.

Years earlier, in 1844, the melody of that song reached people around the world when composer Louis Gottschalk used it to write his famous "La Bamboula: Danse des Nègres, Op.2." Sixty-one years later, African-British composer Samuel Coleridge-Taylor based his composition "The Bamboula" (African Dance) on the same melody. The popularity of "Quan Patate La Cuite" did not end with slavery and was not only sung by black people. It became a part of

Top: Sheet music for "Christy's Minstrels" collection from 1844; Bottom: Sheet music for "Bamboula: Danse des Nègre"

Louis Moreau Gottschalk (1829-1869) was a world-famous musician from New Orleans whose family lived on Rampart Street for a period of time. Gottschalk arranged songs for piano that he learned from his Haitian-born nurse named Sally, many of which gatherers also sang at Congo Square. He became highly successful and toured around the world. One of his most famous compositions was "Bamboula: Danse des Nègre."

New Orleans popular culture into the twentieth century. In 1916, New Orleanian Alice Dunbar-Nelson reported that every child in the city could sing its tune.

The full extent of Congo Square's impact, particularly on the national level, may never be known. The appropriation or use of music and dance of Congo Square for monetary gain was ongoing and unrecorded.

A Place of Protest

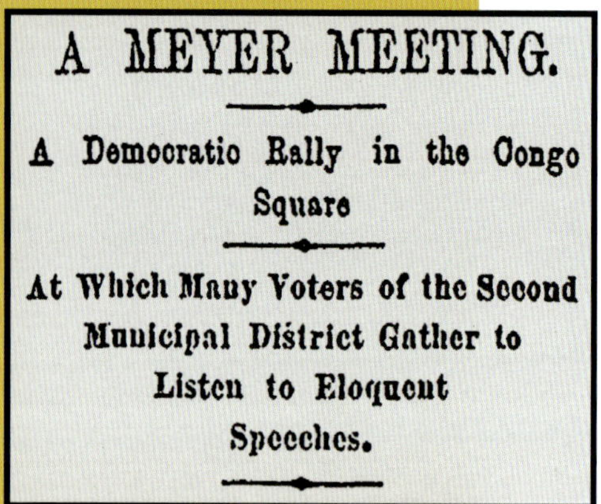

A MEYER MEETING.

A Democratic Rally in the Congo Square

At Which Many Voters of the Second Municipal District Gather to Listen to Eloquent Speeches.

Daily Picayune, October 8, 1890

POLITICAL.

ALL POLITICAL ADVERTISEMENTS MUST BE PAID FOR IN ADVANCE.

Rally! REPUBLICANS! Rally!

A Mass Meeting

OF FIRST DISTRICT VOTERS

IN THE INTEREST OF

McKinley, Hobart and Romain,

WILL BE HELD

AT CONGO SQUARE.

To-Night, Saturday, October 31,

AT 8 O'CLOCK.

Daily Picayune, October 31, 1896

Beginning in the mid 1800s, Congo Square was the choice location for political gatherings, union meetings, and campaign rallies for those seeking public office. Through the years, activism by people of all races has taken place at the Square and protest marches have begun and ended there. One of the largest protests took place in 1867 when over five hundred black people gathered in Congo Square in support of a black man named William Nichols. Police arrested Nichols when he boarded a whites-only, mule-drawn streetcar on Rampart Street near Congo Square and refused to get off. With cases as early as 1862, he was not the first black person to defy the star-car rule, which limited all black people to cars painted with a star. However, his case led to the end of the segregated cars in New Orleans for over thirty years.

The city-run streetcars remained officially integrated until 1902, when a new law overturned the ruling. Six years before that new law, in 1896, the police arrested another black man in New Orleans named Homer Plessy when he boarded a whites-only railcar on the East Louisiana Railroad and refused to exit. Plessy's court case went all the way to the U.S. Supreme Court, where he lost. His defeat meant that the law upheld separate facilities for blacks and whites—as long as they were "equal." The "separate but equal" ruling eventually covered many areas of public life across the country, including restaurants, theaters, restrooms, and public schools, for decades to come.

The long history of resistance and protests that involves Congo Square includes activism during the city's recovery period following Hurricane Katrina. Congo Square served as a starting point for the protest march in 2005 that demanded safe conditions for people who returned to the city and a voice from the people in the rebuilding process. On the second anniversary of the hurricane, in 2007, residents of New Orleans marched from the devastated Lower Ninth Ward to Congo Square to spread their message that politicians had failed to help people return.

National as well as international groups sponsor marches that begin and/or end in Congo Square. In 2006, people gathered there for the local march and rally that protested against the proposed national immigration reform policy. In 2012, a march called SlutWalk, which protested against victim-blaming in cases of sexual assault and which began in Toronto, Canada, was staged in New Orleans and began in Congo Square. The group "Black Youth Project 100 NOLA" led a march from Lee Circle to Congo Square in 2014 to protest the decision not to indict a white police officer in the death of Michael Brown of Ferguson, Missouri. A "Take 'Em Down NOLA" march was also among the many protests that involved Congo Square. In 2016, over two hundred people gathered there and marched to Jackson Square in protest of statues in the city that many believed represented white supremacy.

Congo Square, while known as Beauregard Square, once bore a "white only" sign on one of its trees. At the time it housed a swimming pool, swings, and other playground equipment for neighborhood children as well as a fountain with a wading pool at its center.

A poster for a Take 'Em Down NOLA march

Conclusion

Like windows to the past, the study of Congo Square through primary source documents provides close-up views of past events and shows how those events impacted present-day culture. It reveals Louisiana's connections to countries in parts of Africa and the Caribbean and presents practices and traditions that those locations held in common. It also shows that enslaved Africans contributed more than physical labor to New Orleans and the nation, and it illustrates the significance of the gatherings that took place at the site.

Yet for many people, Congo Square is more than a location. It serves as a reference point for African heritage, African American culture, and black culture in New Orleans. Some see it as proof of the presence and impact of African culture in North America, and some find it to be a source of inspiration for their work. The rich legacy of Congo Square and the many meanings that people derive from it set the location apart from all others. Learning about this national landmark helps us to understand the importance of history as well as the role that it plays in our lives today.

Congo Square by Adewale S. Adenle in the Roots of Music Cultural Sculpture Garden, Louis Armstrong Park, next to Congo Square

Author's Notes

Congo Square is located between St. Ann and St. Peter streets with Rampart Street at its face and the Municipal Auditorium at its rear. The historic landmark now measures 2.35 acres, but it was twice this size before city officials built the auditorium on part of its land in 1930. The plot of land is nestled in the southeast corner of the Louis Armstrong Park, which spreads thirty-two acres and includes the Roots of Music Sculpture Garden, eight sculptures that highlight New Orleans's musical heritage. The Mahalia Jackson Theater and several historic buildings, including Perseverance Hall, the oldest Masonic temple in Louisiana, are also located in the park.

The National Register of Historic Places listed Congo Square in 1993, and the Congo Square Preservation Society, along with other community organizations, erected a historic marker at the site in 1997. The location is known around the world for the music and dances that laid the foundation for the development of jazz. In 2011, a city council ordinance made "Congo Square" the official name of the world-famous landmark.

Today, festivals, concerts, weddings, family reunions, funerals, and political marches are among the numerous events that take place at the site. On Sunday afternoons, New Orleanians of all races, ages, and backgrounds, along with visitors from all parts of the world, gather in Congo Square to sing, dance, and play drums and other instruments. Thanks to members of the Congo Square Preservation Society, the legacy that the gatherers left is kept alive and passed on to the next generation.

PREHISTORIC

Native Americans lived on the land and some tribes celebrated their corn festivals in the area that is now Congo Square.

1660S

Spanish and French explorers entered the territory.

1682

La Salle claimed the territory for France and named the new colony Louisiana after King Louis XIV.

1699

Iberville built a settlement for the colony in the vicinity of present-day Biloxi. Iberville and Bienville explored the area that would become New Orleans.

1718

Bienville founded New Orleans and arranged to bring enslaved Africans to Louisiana.

1719

First two slave ships arrived in Louisiana.

1720S

Le Page du Pratz witnessed enslaved Africans singing, dancing, buying, and selling on different plantations in the colony.

1763

Spanish rule began.

1766

The first Spanish governor arrived.

1803

American rule began.

1817

A city ordinance restricted gathering places. Congo Square eventually became the only Sunday gathering place for enslaved people.

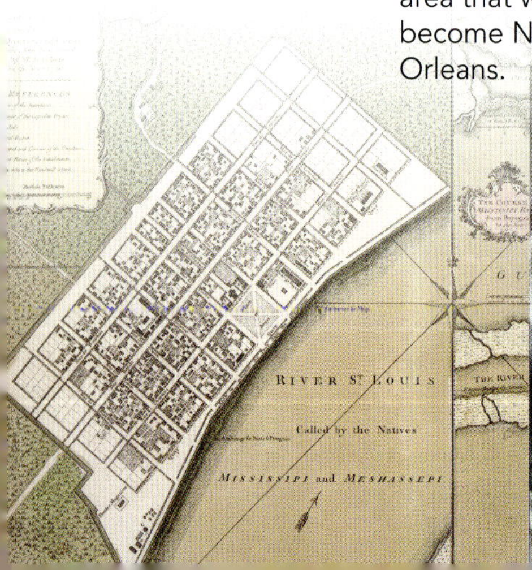

Timeline of Events

1845

City Ordinance re-instated the dances in Congo Square.

1850

A city ordinance named the location Place d'Armes.

1864

Black people celebrated the Emancipation Proclamation in Congo Square.

1893

A city ordinance made Beauregard Square the official name of the location.

1949

First jazz festival was held in Congo Square.

1970

First New Orleans Jazz and Heritage Festival was held in Congo Square.

1993

National Register of Historic Places listed Congo Square.

1997

Congo Square received a historic marker.

2011

A city ordinance made "Congo Square" the official name of the location.

2012

UNESCO (United Nations Education and Scientific and Cultural Organization) launched the first International Jazz Day in Congo Square.

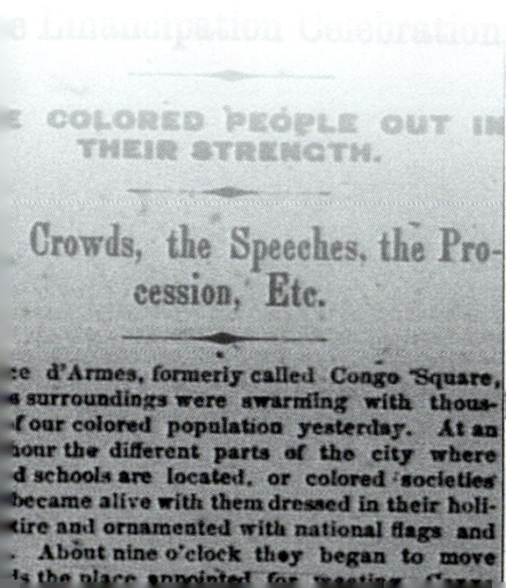

e Emancipation Celebration

E COLORED PEOPLE OUT IN THEIR STRENGTH.

Crowds, the Speeches, the Procession, Etc.

ce d'Armes, formerly called Congo Square,
s surroundings were swarming with thous-
f our colored population yesterday. At an
hour the different parts of the city where
d schools are located, or colored societies
became alive with them dressed in their holi-
tire and ornamented with national flags and
. About nine o'clock they began to move
s the place appointed for meeting ...

On Sunday, July 30, 2017, the Congo Square Preservation Society unveiled the twenty-year-old Congo Square historic marker refurbished in red.

Glossary

African Diaspora	communities throughout the world of African-descended people that resulted from the transatlantic slave trade
balaphon (ba-lə-fän)	African instrument made from wood, resembling a xylophone
banza (bon-zah)	African string instrument made from a gourd, predecessor of the banjo
bayou	small, sometimes sluggish, body of water connected to a larger body
calas (kah-lah)	deep-fried rice cakes sprinkled with powdered sugar, resembles beignets
call and response	African singing style that involved a leader and one or more other singers. In this style, the leader sang a phrase and others followed by singing the same or different set phrase. The leader "called" and the followers "responded."
cobblers	those who make and repair shoes
Code Noir	Louisiana law set in 1724
coffle	a line of animals, prisoners, or slaves chained and driven along together
Congo	refers to the dance and other cultural practices that originated with people from the Kongo-Angola region of Central West Africa.
cornet	a shorter and more conical version of the trumpet often used in early New Orleans jazz

Creole (language) — a French-based language that includes elements of French and African languages

dirge — a slow and sad funeral song

drayman — a person who pulls a low, flat-bed wagon used to transport all kinds of goods

emancipation — freeing from slavery

enslave — to make someone a slave

gourd rattle — musical instrument made from a hardened fruit that resembles a squash or pumpkin

griff (m.)
griffe (f.) — person with ancestors of mixed races

improvisation — making up songs or added words on the spot

indigenous — a person or a thing that began in a particular place

kalimba (kah-lim-bah) — African musical instrument played with both thumbs

Kongo — the Central West African country and its people

maroons — enslaved people who escaped and lived in isolated communities

mulatto (m.)
mulatress (f.) — person with ancestors of mixed races

nkisi — spirits or something that holds spirits, commonly an animal tail

ordinance — a law set by city officials

ornamentation — making voices or instruments slide from one note to another and adding trills to the melody

panpipe	a wind instrument made from hollow cane or bamboo of graduated lengths
petty marketing	buying and selling on a small scale
picayune	a Spanish coin that was small in size and worth very little
pillory device	used for public humiliation and punishment
portage	a path or route used for carrying goods to and fro
pralines	a candy made from readily available ingredients in Louisiana like sugar, butter, cream, and pecans.
quadrilles	A dance performed in Europe and its colonies, involving four couples, similar to the square dance
runaway ad	an advertisement placed in the newspaper about an enslaved person who has run away from his/her owner
sankofa	a West African symbol meaning to "go back and get it" and to "learn from the past." Seen as a bird with its head turned backwards, often taking an egg off its back, or a heart shape, which is commonly seen in ironwork.
second line	people who follow the band and members of the parading club—the main or first line.
ship manifest	a list of the people and/or items on a ship
tignon	a handkerchief used by enslaved women and free women of color to wrap their heads, in compliance with New Orleans city ordinances.
wares	items for sale

The ancestor tree is one of several names in oral history for the largest, and perhaps oldest, tree in the square.

Image Credits

Cover:
left, Woman in Congo Square, courtesy The Historic New Orleans Collection, acc. No. 1977.79.19; center, Young drummers in Congo Square, photographed by author; right, Calinda dance, painting by François Aimé Louis Dumoulin, public domain.

Introduction:
viii, Reproduction of 1845 map of New Orleans, courtesy Thomas Hunt, 2005; ix top, Runaway ad for Sainville, *Daily Picayune,* March 27, 1856; ix right, Sankofa graphic, courtesy of Center for Louisiana Studies; x, Reproduction of 1845 map of New Orleans, courtesy Thomas Hunt, 2005; xi top, Woman in Congo Square, courtesy The Historic New Orleans Collection, acc. No. 1977.79.19; xi bottom, St. Louis Hotel slave block, photographed by Detroit Publishing Co., courtesy of the Library of Congress.

Chapter 1
2, The Louisiana Purchase Projection Sources, courtesy of Portland State University, public domain; 3, *Desseins de Sauvages de Plusieurs Nations, Nlle Orleans,* gift of the estate of Belle J. Bushnell, courtesy the Peabody Museum of Archaeology and Ethnology, Harvard University, PM# 41-72-10/20; 4 top, Map showing Indian portage, courtesy The Historic New Orleans Collection, acc. no. 1947.10.i-iii; 4 bottom, Historic marker for the founding of New Orleans, photographed by J.R. Thomason; 5, Map of New Orleans and Vicinity Fort Ferdinand, courtesy The Historic New Orleans Collection; 6 top, painting by Thure de Thulstrup, public domain; 6 bottom, photograph of Carondelet Canal, courtesy of the Library of Congress; 7, Map of New Orleans, courtesy of Center for Louisiana Studies; 8, "Military Review," *Daily Picayune,* August 5, 1854; 9 top, Jordan Noble's drum, courtesy Neal Auction House; 9 bottom, Jordan Noble photograph, courtesy The Historic New Orleans Collection, acc. no. 58-101-L.3.1; 10 left, "The Emancipation Celebration," *The Era,* June 12, 1864; 10 right, Handwritten Emancipation Proclamation, courtesy of the Library of Congress; 11 top, "Grand Celebration of the Fourth July," *Daily Picayune,* June 30, 1853; 11 bottom, Robinson atlas of New Orleans Treme and Old Basin neighborhood (1883) courtesy of New Orleans Notarial Archives; 12 top, Beauregard Square (1917), courtesy The Historic New Orleans Collection, acc. no. 179.325.5821;

12 bottom, "Ratification Meeting at Beauregard Square," *Daily Picayune*, October 2, 1899; 13, View of Congo Square and Jeff F. X. Municipal Auditorium, photographed by J.R. Thomason; 14, View of Congo Square ground, photographed by J.R. Thomason; 15 top, A plan of the city of Philadelphia (1776), courtesy of the Library of Congress; 15 bottom, George Washington Cable, public domain.

Chapter 2

18, Stowage of the British slave ship *Brookes*, courtesy of the Library of Congress Rare Book and Special Collections Division; 19 top, "Creole Slave for Sale," *Times Picayune* January 14, 1857; 19 bottom, Slave coffle, courtesy 'Wellcome Library, London; 20, Map of African Regions of Slave Trade, courtesy of Center for Louisiana Studies; 21, Toussaint Louverture, public domain; 22, *Attack and take of the Crête-à-Pierrot*, by Auguste Raffet, public domain; 23, Map of the Gulf of Mexico and surrounding countries, public domain; 24, Slave coffle passing the capitol, courtesy of the Library of Congress; 25 top, St. Louis Hotel, courtesy The Historic New Orleans Collection, acc. no. 1974.25.23.4; 25 bottom, Historic marker for Solomon Northup, photographed by J.R. Thomason; 26, People hiding in swamp, courtesy of the Library of Congress; 27 top, Runaway ad for Lavinia, *Daily Picayune*, November 27, 1849; 28 top, Runaway ad for Betsy, *Daily Picayune*, February 20, 1852; 28 bottom, "Harboring A Slave," *Daily Picayune*, April 30, 1852; 29 top, Enslaved female field hand, sketch by E.W. Kemble, from *Century Magazine*, public domain; 29 bottom, Cutting sugar cane, courtesy of the Library of Congress; 30, Card advertisement for slave sale, courtesy of J. W. Boazman, Natchez Trace Collection, Ephemera Collection, NTC_0305a_The Dolph Briscoe Center for American History, The University of Texas at Austin; 31 top left, Illustration from *Harper's Weekly*, courtesy The Historic New Orleans Collection, acc. no. 2002.32.8; 31 top right and bottom, "Plan of 2 Lots & Buildings, 1st District" Pietro Gualdi, April 14, 1855, courtesy Dale N. Atkins, Clerk of Civil District Court, Parish of Orleans; 32, "Five Mechanics for Sale," *Daily Picayune*, December 24, 1852; 33, Southern Pacific Railroad ad, *Daily Picayune*, May 19, 1861; 34, Painting of free woman of color, courtesy The Historic New Orleans Collection, acc. no. 1985.212; 35, Letter of emancipation, courtesy the Louisiana Collection, Tulane University, New Orleans; 36 top, Mrs. Juliet Noel Toussaint, FWC, courtesy the New York Historical Society, Object Number: 1920.5; 36 bottom, Unidentified woman with tignon, courtesy Louisiana State Museum; 37 top, "Congo Square," *The Daily Picayune*, December 22, 1848; 37 bottom, Congo Square, photographed by Georges Mungier, courtesy the Louisiana State Museum.

Chapter 3

40, picayune coin, public domain; 41 top, Code Noir, courtesy the Louisiana Collection, Tulane University, New Orleans; 41 bottom, Sisters of the Holy Family, courtesy of the Library of Congress; 42 both, courtesy the Louisiana Collection, Tulane University, New Orleans; 43, Runaway ad for Pelagie and Pierre, *Daily Picayune*, March 5, 1841; 44, Slave manifest, from ancestry.com; 45 top, Men working among barrels of sugar, courtesy of the Library of Congress; 45 bottom, *Giant Steamboats of New Orleans*, by Hippolyte Sebron (1853), public domain; 46, Parlange Plantation, courtesy of the Library of Congress; 47 top, Slave quarters at Magnolia Plantation, courtesy of the Library of Congress; 47 bottom, Slave quarters in New Orleans French Quarter, courtesy The Historic New Orleans Collection, acc. no. 1985.120.12; 48, Runaway slave icon by Bernarda Bryson, courtesy of the Library of Congress; 49 top, Runaway ad for Charlotte, *The Daily Picayune*, June 2, 1840; 49 bottom, Runaway ad for Caroline, *The Daily Picayune*, May 5, 1849; 50, Jailed slave ad, *Daily Crescent*, December 4, 1851; 51 top, *Vue d'une Rue du Faubourg Ste. Marie, Nelle Orleans* (1821), by Felix Achille de Beaupoil, Marquis de Saint-Aulaire, courtesy The Historic New Orleans Collection, acc. no. 1937.2.3; 51 bottom, "Learning is Wealth" photograph, courtesy of the Library of Congress.

Chapter 4

54, 1845 Ordinance, courtesy Louisiana Division/City Archives, New Orleans Public Library; 55 top, "Scenes in Congo Square," *The Daily Picayune*, June 24, 1845; 55 bottom, Couple dancing, sketch by E.W. Kemble, from *Century Magazine*, public domain; 56 top, Boy blowing the quills, sketch by E. W. Kemble, from *Century Magazine*; 56 bottom, Sketches of musical instruments, from the original manuscript journals of Benjamin Latrobe, courtesy the Maryland Historical Society, Baltimore; 57 from left to right: Barrel drum, courtesy the Louisiana State Museum, photographed by J. R. Thomason; balaphon, courtesy of Segenon Kone, photographed by the author; Kalimba, mbira, likembe, courtesy Dr. Robert Gex Collection, Southern University of New Orleans Archives; Carved drum, courtesy the Louisiana State Museum, made by Titos Sampa, photographed by Danny Kadar; Flute made from bamboo, from the author's collection, photographed by J. R. Thomason; Slit drum, courtesy the Summers Multi-Ethnic Institute of Arts, photographed by J. R. Thomason; Gourd rattles, from the author's collection, photographed by J. R. Thomason; Mule's jawbone, courtesy the Summers Multi-Ethnic Institute of Arts, photographed by J. R. Thomason; Panpipes, courtesy of Shutterstock; Banza: from the author's collection, photographed by J. R. Thomason; 59, Music notation, from *Creole Songs from New Orleans* by Clara Gottschalk Peterson (New Orleans, LA: L. Grunewald Co., 1909) courtesy Howard Tilton Library, Tulane University, New Orleans; 60, A fiddler, sketch by E. W. Kemble, from *Century Magazine*, public domain; 61, Calinda dance, painting by François Aimé Louis Dumoulin, public domain; 62 top, *Capoeira* or "Dance of War," by Johann Moritz Rugendas, public domain; 62 bottom, Militeri Tucker Concepcion, dancer and William "Billy T" Tucker, drummer, photographer Marisol Diaz; 63, Sketch "The Bamboula," by E.W. Kemble, from *Century Magazine*, courtesy The Historic New Orleans Collection, acc. no. 1974.25.23.54; 64 both, William Henry Lane illustration and playbill, public domain; 65, Danny "Slapjazz" Barber and Sekani Thomas, photographed by Sherwood Chen; 67 top, Diviner from Katanga, Congo (2006), courtesy Jacques Jangoux, JNGX0841; 67 bottom, Painting of Marie Laveau, courtesy Louisiana State Museum; 68, Woman selling pralines, photographed by Georges Mugnier, courtesy the Louisiana State Museum 09813.22; 69, "A Marchande des Calas," sketch by E.W. Kemble from *Century Magazine*, courtesy The Historic New Orleans Collection, acc. n. 1974.25.20.126; 70, Plate of calas, public domain.

Chapter 5

74, Musical notation "Los Companillas" by Basile Bares, courtesy Xavier University of Louisiana Archives and Special Collections; 75 top, Runaway ad for Edmond, *The Daily Picayune*, September 11, 1847; 75 bottom, Runaway ad for Harrison, *Daily Picayune*, May 8, 1854; 76, Cartoon from *The Mascot*, November 15, 1890, public domain; 77, Oscar "Papa" Celestin, courtesy the Louisiana State Museum; 77 bottom, Jelly Roll Morton, courtesy the Jazz Hogan Archives, Tulane University; 78 left, Michael White, photo by Braden Piper, courtesy of Basin Street Records; 78 right, "Jelly Roll Blues," public domain; 78 bottom, Wynton Marsalis, courtesy Jazz at Lincoln Center; 79 top, Louis Armstrong at New Orleans International Jazz Festival, 1968, courtesy Jules Cahn Collection at The Historic New Orleans Collection, acc. no. 2000.78.1.1546 and The Louis Armstrong Educational Foundation; 79 bottom, International Jazz Day, courtesy Skip Bolen/WireImage; 80, Black Men of Labor Social Aid and Pleasure Club lead jazz funeral, photographed by the author; 81 top, Brass band, photographed by author; 81 bottom, Sons of Hope and Annual Parade, public domain; 82, Lady Buck Jumpers Social Aid and Pleasure Club, photographed by Freddye Hill; 83, Young Men Olympian Junior Benevolent Association (YMO) lead jazz funeral, photographed by Freddye Hill; 84, Women in Nigeria dancing with handkerchiefs, courtesy Shutterstock; 85 top, "African Teenager Dance Sing (2006)," courtesy Jacques Jangoux; 85 bottom, Dancers in New Orleans waving handkerchiefs as they second-line, photographed by Freddye Hill; 86, Wild Red Flame Mardi Gras Indians, photographed by the author; 87, Black Mohawk Mardi Gras Indians, photographed by the author; 88, Loretta S. Harrison, photo courtesy of Stephen Smith Jr.; 89, "Christy's Minstrels" and "Bamboula" sheet music, public domain; 90 top, *Daily Picayune*, October 8, 1890; 90 bottom, *Daily Picayune*, October 31, 1896; 91, Take 'Em Down NOLA poster, permission granted from Take 'Em Down NOLA.

Back matter:

94, Congo Square sculpture, photographed by J.R. Thomason; 98, Congo Square historic marker, photographed by Mikelle Evans; 102, Ancestor tree, photographed by Melvin I. Evans.

Bibliography

Blockson, Charles L. *African Americans in Pennsylvania, a History and Guide.* Baltimore: Black Classic Press, 1994.

Cable, George Washington. *The Dance in Place Congo & Creole Slave Songs.* New Orleans: Synoeceosial Farukvon Turk, 1976.

Christy, Edwin Pearce. *Christy's Plantation Melodies, No. 4.* Philadelphia: Fisher & Brothers, 1854.

Courlander, Harold. "Musical Instruments of Haiti." *The Musical Quarterly* 27, no. 3 (1941): 371-83.

———. "Musical Instruments of Cuba." *The Musical Quarterly* 28, no. 2 (1942): 227-40.

Creecy, James. *Scenes in the South.* Philadelphia: Lippincott & Company, 1860.

Dunbar-Nelson, Alice. "People of Color in Louisiana: Part II." *The Journal of Negro History* 1, no. 4 (1916): 361-76.

Du Pratz, Antoine Le Page. *The History of Louisiana.* Edited by Joseph G. Tregle Jr. Baton Rouge: Louisiana State University Press, 1975.

Evans, Estwick. "A Pedestrian Tour of 4000 Miles in Western and Southwestern States and Territories during the Winter & Spring of 1818." In *Early Western Travels, 1748-1846,* Vol. VIII, edited by Reuben Gold Thwaites. Cleveland: A. H. Clark, 1904.

Evans, Freddi W. *Congo Square: African Roots in New Orleans.* Lafayette: University of Louisiana at Lafayette Press, 2011.

Floyd, Samuel. "Black Music in the Circum-Caribbean." *American Music* 17, no. 1 (Spring, 1999): 1-38.

Grattan, H. P. "The Origin of the Christy's Minstrels." In *The Theatre—A Month Review of the Drama, Music, and the Fine Arts.* Vol. V (1882): 129-33.

Hall, Gwendolyn Midlo. *Africans in Colonial Louisiana*. Baton Rouge: Louisiana State University Press, 1922.

———. *Slavery and African Ethnicities in the Americas*. Chapel Hill: University of North Carolina Press, 2005.

Hare, Maude Cuney. *Six Creole Folk Songs*. New York: Carl Fischer, 1921.

Ingraham, Joseph Holt. *The South-West By a Yankee*. Vol. I. New York: Harper & Brothers, 1835.

Johnson, Jerah. *Congo Square in New Orleans*. New Orleans: Louisiana Landmarks Society, 1995. Originally published as "New Orleans' Congo Square: An Urban Setting for Early Afro-American Culture Formation." *Louisiana History* 32 (Spring 1991): 117-57.

King, Grace. *New Orleans, the Place and the People*. New York: Macmillan Company, 1899.

Knight, Henry Cogswell [Arthur Singleton]. *Letters from the South and West*. Boston: Richardson and Lord, 1824.

LaChance, Paul. "The 1809 Immigration of Saint-Dominique Refugees." In *The Road Louisiana: The Saint-Domingue Refugees, 1792-1809*, edited by Carl A. Brasseaux and Glen R. Conrad, 245-84. Lafayette: Center for Louisiana Studies, 1992.

Latrobe, Henry Benjamin. *The Journals of Benjamin Latrobe 1799- 1820 From Philadelphia to New Orleans*. Vol. 3. Edited by Edward C. Carter II, John C. Van Horne, and Lee W., Formwalt. New Haven: Yale University Press, 1980.

Le Blanc de Villeneufve, Paul Louis. *The Festival of the Young Corn or The Heroism of Poucha-Houmma*. Lafayette: University of Southwestern Louisiana, 1964.

Leovy, Henry Jefferson. *The Laws and General Ordinances of the City of New Orleans*. New Orleans: E. C. Wharton, 1857.

Long, Ellen Call. *Florida Breezes or Florida, New and Old*. Jacksonville: Ashmead Brothers, 1883.

Mbiti, John. *African Religions and Philosophy*. Portsmouth, NH: Heinemann Educational Publishers, 1969.

Medley, Keith Weldon. "New Orleans Congo Square, African Seeds in American Soil." *New Orleans Tribune* (August 1986).

Moreau De Saint-Mery, Mederic-Louis-Elie. *Dance*. Translated by Lily and Baird Hastings. Philadelphia: A Dance Horizon Publication, 1976.

Nickerson, Camille Lucie. *Africo-Creole Music in Louisiana*. Master's Thesis, Oberlin Conservatory of Music, 1932.

Nketia, J.H. Kwabena. *The Music of Africa*. New York: W.W. Norton & Company, 1974.

Peterson, Clara Gottschalk. *Creole Songs From New Orleans in the Negro Dialect*. New Orleans: L. Grunewald, c.1909.

Schultz, Christian. *Travels on an Island Voyage*. Vol. II. New York: Isaac Riley, 1810.

Schweninger, Loren, ed. *The Autobiography of James Thomas: From Tennessee Slave to St. Louis Entrepreneur.* Columbia: University of Missouri Press, 1984.

Sublette, Ned. *The World That Made New Orleans—From Spanish Silver to Congo Square*. Chicago: Lawrence Hill Books, 2008.

Thompson, Robert Farris. "When the Saints Go Marching In: Kongo Louisiana, Kongo New Orleans." In *Resonance from the Past: African Sculpture from the New Orleans Museum of Art*, edited by Frank Herreman. New York: Museum of African Art, 2005.

Thorpe, Edward. *Black Dance*. New York: The Overlook Press, 1990.

Toledano, Roulhac and Mary Louise Christovich. *New Orleans Architecture*. Vol. 6, *Faubourg Treme and the Bayou Road*. Gretna: Pelican Publishing Company, 1980.

Index

D

E

F

G

T

U

V

W

Y

Z